# Good to GREAT GOLF

## Shatter Your Lowest Round with Absolute Mental Focus

## Dr. Rob Gilbert
## John Sikes Jr.

**LEGACY** Publishing Services
1883 Lee Road • Winter Park, FL 32789
www.LegacyPublishingServices.com

Published by:
**LEGACY PUBLISHING SERVICES, INC.**
1883 Lee Road
Winter Park, Florida 32789
LegacyPublishingServices.com

Copyright © 2006, 2008 by John Sikes, Jr., Dr. Robert Gilbert
ISBN 0-9776777-7-X
Cover Design by Gabriel H. Vaughn

For comments to the author, scheduling interviews or speaking engagements, contact through the *authors'* page at www.LegacyPublishingServices.com.

For more information about the book and other golf tips visit, www.GoodToGreatGolf.com
or call toll free number, 1-877-GOLF-421.

Printed in United States of America

All rights reserved. Written permission must be secured from the publisher to use or reproduce any part of this book, except for brief critical reviews or articles.

## ACKNOWLEDGMENTS

John Sikes Jr. thanks co-author Dr. Rob Gilbert for his inspiration and blueprint for this book.

To Dennis Coffey for his vast knowledge of golf history and the game itself.

To the following sport psychologists who have supported the work of Championship Performance for the last 10 years: Dr. Ken Ravizza, Dr. Alan Goldberg, Dr. Harvey Dulberg, Dr. Jack Stark, and Dr. Kay Porter.
www.championshipperform.com

To my friends and family especially Kate, Hope, and Joshua.

To God for His mercy and grace.

## DEDICATION

*This book is dedicated to the work of the International Justice Mission. (IJM.org)*

*20 percent of the profits of this book sold directly through the goodtogreatgolf.com web site will go to support this Christian based relief organization who work on behalf of the oppressed around the world, particularly children at risk of sexual exploitation.*

**IJM serves a Four-Fold Purpose:**

*1) Victim Relief-* Relieve the victim of the abuse currently being committed.

*2) Perpetrator Accountability -* Bring accountability and just consequences under the law to the specific perpetrator(s) of abuse.

*3) Structural Prevention -* Prevent the abuse from being committed against others who are at risk by strengthening community factors that are likely to deter potential oppressors, reduce the vulnerability of at-risk populations and empower local authorities to stop such abuses.

*4) Victim Aftercare-* Provide access to services to help victims transition to their new lives and to encourage long-term success.

# Table of Contents

**Introduction:** A Golf Story You Will Never Forget

**Chapter 1:** The Overnight Success Principle .................. 13

**Chapter 2:** The One Tactic to Improve Your Golf Game Immediately ....................... 21

**Chapter 3:** Release Your Mental Emergency Break ........ 33

**Chapter 4:** The Killer Attitude that Destroys Your Great Round ......................................... 45

**Chapter 5:** The Often Overlooked Key to Shooting a Lower Score ..................................... 51

**Chapter 6:** Proven Concentration Techniques to Achieve the Focus of Champions ................. 57

**Chapter 7:** Practice Habits to Revolutionize the Way You Play the Game ................................. 67

**Chapter 8:** Visualizing Your Next Best Round to Make it a Reality ............................................ 79

**Chapter 9:** Ultimate Golf Psychology: 3 Sure Fire Methods to Lower Your Score ........................ 87

- Goal-Setting Strategies to Improve Your Game Now and Forever
- Slumpbusting
- The Psychology of Finishing Strong

**Chapter 10:** Decision or Action: In the End, It's Up to You ................................. 99

**Chapter 11:** 36 Power Statements to Play Your Best Golf Today ...................... 103

## A GOLF STORY YOU WILL NEVER FORGET

I'm Dr. Rob Gilbert and I want to share a golf story with you that you will never forget.

An officer was captured during the Vietnam War after his plane was shot down over enemy territory. He ended up spending years of confinement in a prisoner of war camp.

As an officer, he wasn't tortured, but he was forced to spend nearly every hour inside a cell with no books, television, or other distractions to take his mind off his captivity.

Sitting alone in his cell, the officer came up with a unique way to pass the time. As a serious recreational golfer, he thought about the fun times he had on his favorite course back home. Soon, he developed a more intricate routine. He would play the game in his mind... shot by shot, hole by hole.

Month after month he would play the same course over and over, each time seeing in his mind how he would execute individual shots at each hole in sequence, including putting once on the green.

Since he had no place to go, in his mind he took every step on his way to the ball – experiencing the fragrance of trees and freshly trimmed grass along the way. It took him just as long in imaginary time as it would have in reality. He repeated this exercise for several hours a day for years.

The officer was a decent player, but nothing special. He would typically struggle to break 90. Upon his release, one of the first things he wanted to do was play that favorite course once again. The first time back a remarkable thing happened.

He ended up shooting a 74, by far his best performance ever. Now, the entire time he spent in prison he didn't practice his swing once with a real golf club. But his mental practice had attuned his body to execute his swing to perfection for his level of talent.

"Golf is a game that is played on a 5 inch course - the space between your ears."

— Bobby Jones

## THE OVERNIGHT SUCCESS PRINCIPLE

For the last 25 years I've been teaching sport psychology at Montclair State University. During that time, I've helped thousands of athletes – from high school to professionals – *do their best when it means the most.*

Tomorrow you will play another round of golf. It could be a qualifier for the professional tour or a typical weekend foursome with some of your buddies. Let me ask you four questions:

1) Suppose you hit 500 shots on the range today. Will you have a better swing tomorrow?

Probably not.

2) Suppose you stay up all night putting on an indoor practice green. Will you be a better putter tomorrow?

Certainly not.

3) Suppose you spend all day practicing the areas of your game that are your weakest. Will you be more skilled tomorrow?

Once again, no.

4) But…can you have a better attitude tomorrow than you do right now?

Absolutely!

You can't improve your basic swing or golf skills overnight, but you can dramatically improve your attitude. In other words, between tonight and tomorrow, you can go from a losing attitude to a winning attitude.

That's exactly what this book will do for you. This book will show you precisely what to do so you can…

…have the mind-set of a winner to lower your score the next time out on the course.

But hold on! If you want to have the mindset of a winner, there is one thing you absolutely cannot do.
There is one thing that will guarantee failure.
There is one thing that will destroy you.
There is one thing that will rob you of any chance you have of winning tomorrow.

The one thing is…

You can't lose hope. Why? Because once you lose hope - you lose all your chances of winning. If you feel it's hopeless because the guys you are playing with have lower handicaps and are such good players - you'll lose. If you feel it's hopeless because you're so nervous that "you can't putt worth a darn" - you'll lose.

Here's the truth: In golf, there are no hopeless situations.

My first goal in this book is to give you hope. Let me tell you a story about the greatest underdog of all time. He could have lost hope but he didn't. It was way back during biblical times and David was to go on the field of battle the next day to fight a gargantuan named Goliath.

David was getting ready to go to bed when three of his friends came into his tent to make a condolence call. Basically, they told

David that it was nice knowing him because they knew he was going to get killed.

"Wait a second," David said. "You think Goliath's going to win?"

His friends nodded.

"No way," David said.

"How can you be so confident?," one of his friends asked.

"Simple, I have my slingshot and Goliath's so big- how can I possibly miss!"

How was David able to be so positive?

Because David knew that...

...The best fighter never wins.

Let me explain.

Would you have bet money that David would beat Goliath? It was a seemingly hopeless situation.

- Goliath was bigger.
- Goliath was stronger.
- Goliath was fiercer.

In other words, Goliath was better than David in every respect. But Goliath lost because even though he was better, David fought better that day. You see...

The best golfer doesn't win. The golfer who plays the best always wins. It doesn't matter who can crush the ball 350 yards off the tee - all that matters is who plays better. It doesn't matter who is better - all that matters is who plays better that day, during that round. The golfer who is better doesn't win. The golfer who plays better does.

David was the first in a long line of winners who weren't "supposed to win." And if you think the story of David and Goliath is just an ancient bible parable, let me share two examples of modern day Davids beating all the odds.

It was during the 1913 U.S. Open that a little known amateur named Francis Quimet shocked the golfing world at the time by beating 6 time British Open champion Harry Vardon.

This 20 year old caddie, playing in the shadows of the course he worked at as a child and teenager, forced a play-off with an exceptional final day performance.

Taking the advice from his idol Vardon who once said that there are only two types of golfers – those who keep their nerves about them and win championships and those that don't – Quimet kept his composure with the whole golfing world watching him. Writers at the time said Quimet was a model of poise under pressure.

When he reflected back on his mind-set on that final day 50 years later, Quimet described what mental toughness was all about with this reply: *"I wasn't thinking of being poised or not. I was thinking of hitting every ball as well as I could. I wanted every shot to be as perfect as it could be."*

---

If you saw the movie Miracle about the 1980 U.S. Olympic hockey team, they were supposed to lose to the invincible Russians. But the United States won.

Why? Even though the Russians were the better team, the United States was the team that played better.

Here's a little piece of trivia:

Three days before the Olympic games began in 1980, at an exhibition game at Madison Square Garden in New York City, the same two teams met. The Russians beat the Americans by a score of 10-3. Al Michaels, who covered the game as a sportscaster for NBC, reported the Americans were so outclassed that, "They were lucky they didn't lose by a score of 20-0!"

After that game, United States coach Herb Brooks knew that his first job was not to let his team lose hope. This is what Brooks told his team before they played the Russians again: "Great moments are born from great opportunity. That's what you have earned here tonight. If we played the Russians 10 times, they would probably win 9. But not tonight. Tonight we skate with them. Tonight we stay with them. Tonight we shut them down. Why? Because we can. Tonight we are the greatest hockey team in the world. You were meant to be here. You were born to be a hockey player. This moment is yours."

Ten days after that humiliating loss, the U.S. played the Russians for real in the Olympic tournament. Final score:

United States 4
Soviet Union 3

My first goal is to give you the same type of hope on the golf course that Herb Brooks gave his team and the same hope that Francis Quimet gave amateur golfers everywhere.

My second goal is to make sure you lower your score the next time you play a round of golf - whether you are "supposed to" or not. Starting right now, remember that no matter who you're competing against, no matter what happens—there is always hope.

This acronym will help you to remember what we've just been talking about:

# H.O.P.E.
## Hold On Possibilities Exist

Watch the two movies I just described back to back the week before you play your next round of golf. *The Greatest Game Ever Played* is the story of Francis Quimet and the 1913 U.S. Open championship. *"Miracle"* chronicles the U.S. Olympic Hockey team's incredible 1980 defeat of the Russians. You will have hope.

# GREAT GOLF Tip ①

## Profiles in Mental Toughness:
*Family Helped Change Mental Attitude*
— VJ Singh

After missing the cut for the 1998 Masters tournament, VJ Singh had a conversation with his wife that changed his entire mental attitude. After he complained on the ride home that he would never be able to play well at Augusta National, his wife scolded him by saying, "With an attitude like that, you might as well pack it in because you will never succeed thinking like that."

"The first year I went, I hated the greens and I found the atmosphere so tense. I didn't enjoy it, and each year I've been back, I hated it even more," Singh noted.

But after the 1998 conversation he vowed, "I'm going to go there and love the place, love the environment, love the greens. To play well there, you've got to have the right attitude. When I'm walking between shots, that's when I get the most nervous butterflies. I look around and I'm not at ease. But when I'm over the ball, I'm comfortable. That's key."

The greens had destroyed his chances in the past, but not this year. He three-putted only twice and never unraveled. He reverted to a cross-handed, or left-hand-low grip, at the urging of his wife - another great suggestion.

"That stopped me from worrying if I'm going to pull it or push it," Singh said. "I'm just trying to enjoy putting. I try to tell myself when I walk on the green that 'You're going to enjoy this putt.'" Singh kept reminding himself to enjoy the game. With his new attitude came a breakthrough performance.

A final key came from an unlikely source – Singh's 9 year old son. On the final day of the 2000 Masters, he taped a note to his father's golf bag that read, "Poppa, trust your swing."

"I think my attitude change was a big boost," Singh said after winning the 2000 Masters Tournament, his first victory at Augusta National.

"I get nervous with every shot."

—Tiger Woods

"I am the toughest player mentally."

—Tiger Woods

## THE ONE TACTIC TO IMPROVE YOUR GOLF GAME
## <u>IMMEDIATELY</u>

Golf can be incredibly frustrating. Just look at some of the greatest players in the last ten years and some of their famous collapses to see what I'm talking about. We don't like to call it "choking", but what other word would you use to describe the following instances?:

- Seve Ballesteros four putts on the 16$^{th}$ hole during the 1988 Masters dooming his chances for a victory.

- Greg Norman begins the final day of the 1996 Masters with a six stroke lead. In what has been called the most humiliating collapse in golf history, Norman shoots a 78 to lose by five strokes.

- Jean Van de Velde blows a three shot lead by unwisely deciding not to lay up on the final hole of the British Open. His ball would end up in a creek. It was mental breakdown on two fronts that spelled his demise: One for making a poor decision and second from making a poor swing.

There are two things that can destroy your performance tomorrow if you handle them wrong. They are…worry and fear.

I'll bet that one of the reasons you are reading this book right now is that you're concerned about what might happen the next time you play a competitive round.

Right now I want you to write down, on the following blank lines, five things that worry you about tomorrow. Don't hold back. Write down your big worries and your small ones.

Nobody will ever see this list unless you show it to them. Here's the trick: Don't think a lot about it - just write. So what's worrying you...

1._____
2._____
3._____
4._____
5._____

Here's something you need to know... it's okay to be worried!

*(In other words, don't worry about being worried.)*

Everybody worries. The question is: What do most people worry about?

They worry about what people will say about them and they worry about what their friends and fellow golfers will think about them.

Here is a story about a young girl who could care less about what others would say or think about her...

Nobody thought that she was the smartest fourth grader. She wasn't the most musical, athletic, or artistic. But this little girl was the world's most confident fourth grader.

One day, the art teacher came into class and said, "Today you can paint, draw or finger paint anything you want."

The world's most confident fourth grader shot her hand up into the air and asked, "Can I draw a picture of God?"

Through her chuckles, the teacher said, "Nobody knows what God looks like."

With all the confidence in the world, the little girl said, "Oh, they will when I'm done!"

Now that's a winning attitude!

Muhammed Ali, one of the greatest athletes of all time, made the same point...

"In order to be a great champion, you have to believe that you are the best. And if you don't – pretend that you are!"

Tomorrow you have to do what this little girl did. Tomorrow you have to take Muhammed Ali's advice.

Care a little less about what other golfers will think about you. Care a little less about what other golfers will say about you.

Just because you might feel worried doesn't mean you have to act worried. Act confident regardless of how you feel.

Let's face it, if a little fourth grader can do it. You can do it too. You can have the round of your life.

So instead of worrying what people will think and say about you, do what the little fourth grader did...Act Confident!

The secret is to be a good actor. Just because you are worried doesn't mean you have to act worried.

Another way of saying this is...

It's alright to have butterflies in your stomach – just get them to fly in formation!

Right now I bet you can act like the most confident person in the world. Let me prove it to you. Suppose I offered you

$1,000,000 if you could act superbly confident for the next 10 minutes? Could you do this? Of course you could.

Remember your A, B, C's…
**Always      Behave      Confidently**.

Let's quickly review:

1. It's OK to be worried. Everybody worries.

2. You can act confident regardless of how you feel.

However, suppose you'd like to act confident, but there's something bothering you that is even worse than being worried.

You're scared of making mistakes on the course!

It's OK to be scared! Some of the greatest athletes of all time did their best when they were scared to death. You can, too!

I have a friend who's been working with professional boxers for years. He knows all the champions. Once I asked him if the great fighters like Ali, Lennox Lewis and Evander Holyfield are as confident in the locker room as they look when they're walking into the ring.

My friend told me that before the fight, these superstars were scared to death. But when they leave the locker room and start walking to the ring, they're acting as if they're confident.

One of the greatest pro basketball players of all time was Bill Russell of the Boston Celtics. Before most games he was so nervous that he threw up. And he still played great!

Remember, it's okay to be scared, just don't act like you are.

Act confident.

How many times do you warm up on the range and feel great only to head over to the first tee full of butterflies in your stomach? You have to take that same positive feeling you had on the range and bring it with you just like those boxers walking into the ring.

So if you're scared, frightened or even panicky, hold on, there's hope.

In the movie "The Legend of Bagger Vance", actor Matt Damon plays the role of Randolph Junuh, a once promising amateur champion who after returning home from World War 1 has lost not only his once incredible golf swing, but his hope in life as well. He is befriended by Bagger Vance, a mysterious stranger who ends up being his caddy in a celebrity match against two of the game's greats – Bobby Jones and Walter Hagen.

As Junuh falls behind 12 strokes on the first day, Vance counsels him on how to find his perfect shot and authentic stroke.

"*You need to get out of your own way,*" Vance tells him. Later in the match, Junuh has almost caught up with some spectacular play. But on the final day, distracted by adoring crowds and his former girlfriend, Junuh hits two poor bunker shots leading to a triple bogey. His confidence sagging, he shanks the next tee shot into the woods.

In the movie's pivotal scene, Junuh tells Vance "I can't do this," as he stares down at his ball with trees surrounding him. Vance's reply was said to offer hope and encouragement at a time of great distress. "You have a choice. It's time to come out of the shadows. You can do this. Now play your game. The only game you were meant to play. Strike the ball and don't hold nothin' back. Now is the time."

Junuh then hits the shot of the match and later finishes in a 3 way tie with the legends (it was only an exhibition match).

Just like Randolph Junuh, you may feel nervous or intimidated but that doesn't mean you have to act scared. You can act confident regardless of how you feel.

Just because you feel a certain way doesn't mean you have to act that way. This means even though you feel scared, you can still act confident.

Act as if it were impossible to fail, even if you are scared, even if you don't believe your next round or next shot will be your best one ever.

Don't let your feelings dictate your actions. Let your actions dictate your feelings.

Most people won't do this because they feel they have to be successful before they can start acting successful.

Absolutely false!!!

They have it backwards. First, start acting successful then you will become successful.

So you don't have to be a champion to start acting like one. As a matter of fact, you can start acting like one right now.

---

Let's look at it this way…

Suppose you're invited to play in a special tournament as the lone amateur. One day during the practice round, Tiger Woods shows up. He starts smashing balls off the tee with power you can only dream of. Later he seems to sink putts with effortless ease.

So of course Tiger can beat you mechanically. But, can you go back to the practice tee and instantly choose to have the attitude, intensity and make the effort of a Tiger Woods? Yes! You can mimic his mental toughness as well.

Attitude, effort and focus of intensity are all a choice!

Here is a losing mindset: "I have to be a great golfer before I can start acting like a great golfer."

Contrast that with this winning mindset: "I can start acting like a great golfer well before I am a great golfer. And I can start acting that way right now!"

So far, we've covered four things...

1. Have hope. Realize that in golf there are no hopeless situations, just players who let themselves lose hope.

2. The best golfer doesn't win. The golfer that plays best does win.

3. It's OK to be worried- just don't act worried.

4. It's OK to be scared, frightened or even panicky- just don't act scared, frightened or panicky. Act confidently.

Here's another example: Rich Beem won a major PGA event with Tiger Woods breathing down his neck back in 2002. Why, when so many others have cracked under pressure, did Beem pull out a victory?

Beem admits that he feared Woods, yet he didn't play scared. The big name golfers have Tiger on the brain and they alter their games. They constantly check the scoreboard. They play as if they have everything to lose.

Not Beem. He played with fun and reckless abandon. Once he even yelled at the ball "c'mon, c'mon" as he ran down the fairway toward the green.

To get rid of his nervousness, he tightened and relaxed his stomach muscles and gulped some Pepto Bismal. It took his mind off his swing and loosened his arms.

He withstood a furious late rush from Tiger by playing like he had nothing to lose. He acted as if he wasn't nervous and pulled off a major tour event upset.

---

Now let me tell you about the secret weapon that former Los Angeles Dodger manager Tommy Lasorda used when he sensed that his players were worried or scared or starting to lose hope. When he felt the team was in an absolutely "must win" situation, he brought in…

…a comedian named Don Rickles.

Rickles' routine is that he makes fun of people. He makes fun of the way they look, the way they act, the way they talk. He makes fun of just everything about them! When he was in the Dodgers locker room, no one escaped his wrath. The more Rickles talked, the more the players laughed. Not only were they laughing - they were laughing at themselves! When Rickles finished his pre-game routine, the Dodgers weren't as worried. They weren't as scared.

**Keep this in mind before you play you next round:**

- When you laugh - you loosen up physically.

- When you loosen up physically - you lighten up mentally.

- When you lighten up mentally - you play better.

**On the opposite side:**

- When you are worried or scared - you tighten up physically.

- When you tighten up physically - you get uptight mentally.

- When you get uptight mentally - you play worse.

Here's a story that perfectly illustrates this point. It was during the 1971 U.S. Open when a young hot shot named Lee Trevino forced an 18 hole play-off with Jack Nicklaus. On the first tee box, Trevino pulls a rubber snake out of his golf bag and tosses it at Nicklaus.

"Hey, this must of come with me all the way from Texas," Trevino said as he laughed before hitting his first shot. He went on to win the event, his first major.

When asked in a press conference before the play-off about how he was going to handle the pressure competing against a living legend like Nicklaus, Trevino jokingly said, "There is no pressure on me. I've got nothing to lose. I'm just a poor Mexican. In fact, my family was so poor – that when somebody threw our dog a bone, he had to call for a fair catch."

This book contains different stories to help loosen you up and play better the next time you are out on the course. Stories loosen you up and inspire you because they give you hope.

***Remember...***

# H.O.P.E.
Hold On Possibilities Exist

One of the ways we get hope is another acronym...

# H.O.P.E
**Hearing Other People's Experiences**
(and being inspired by them)

My goal for any golfer who is reading this book is very simple:

1. After you finish reading it, you will have the right frame of mind in place to help you shoot a lower score. Just like David, Muhammad Ali, Francis Quimet, Randolph Junuh, Rich Beem, the Dodgers and Lee Trevino.

2. The other golfers in your next foursome won't know any of this information and they'll keep making the same old mental mistakes they've always made. Just like Goliath.

**GREAT GOLF Tip 2**

**Profiles in Mental Toughness:**
*"Acting as if"* Sealed Grand Slam Title
— Gary Player

His legendary mental discipline propelled Gary Player to the top ranks of the professional golf world for the last five decades. At 5 feet 7 inches and 150 pounds, he made up for his lack of physical skills with a practice work ethic that would put many of today's tour players to shame. At 29, he was one of the youngest professionals to win all 4 major championships in one year and claim the Grand Slam title.

He said he didn't feel the pressure until he won a third tournament and had to win the U.S. Open to get his fourth. To cope with the pressure, he used a combination of prayer and visualization. Player knew the importance of "acting as if" he was a champion to make it a reality.

According to Player, "I went to St. Louis that year where the U.S. Open was being played and every day I went to a church and I prayed for great patience and courage. I would go down to the scoreboard that listed the names of the champions through the years - 1965 was vacant. I'd stand there for a few minutes everyday and I meditated. I saw my name up there. Gary Player, 1965, Open Champion. It was almost a self-hypnosis."

As a teenager, Player read Norman Vincent Peale's *The Power of Positive Thinking*; a book that transformed his approach to sports. Player was among the first to grasp and apply psychological principles to golf.

He realized early on in his career that it was easy to lose focus and become lethargic or conversely - become overly energetic.

"You've got to try and keep a good balance. I would say to myself, 'Don't get too excited because you never know what's around the corner.' And when I'm not doing well, I say, 'Just keep punching and plugging, because you'll be rewarded.'

Golf is such a humbling game. There's a line in a poem on golf called "*Forgin's Creed*" written by a Scot that goes, 'so many great shots end up in sheer disaster.' But it is how you handle adversity that defines you as a person. I see guys who let the littlest things undo them, undo their confidence, undo their motivation. Get in there and play the game with some courage. It is part of the game to have bad times. Show some courage. Show some patience. Show some determination!"

"Through the learning to read a golf course came an ever sharpening awareness that one's true opponent in every golf contest is never another player, but always the course itself. The only thing a player can control is his own game, so concern about what other competitors may or may not do is both a useless distraction and a waste of energy."

— Jack Nicklaus

## Chapter THREE

**RELEASE YOUR MENTAL EMERGENCY BREAK**

Here's another story to illustrate the point I made in the last chapter. Jim's parents gave him a graduation party where his rich Uncle Paul showed up. He was a multi-millionaire international businessman who was always busy flying around the world making deals. Just before Uncle Paul left, he took Jim aside and asked him how well he thought he was going to do in college.

"Don't worry, Uncle Paul, I'll get by. I'll graduate."

"I want you to do more than graduate," Uncle Paul said. "I want you to graduate with highest honors like I did - it's called 'summa cum laude.' You know, four years from tonight your parents are probably going to have another graduation party for you and I want to give you something special that night if you graduate with highest honors. What do you want?"

"A car would be nice," Jim said.

"What kind of car?"

"Anything that moves," Jim joked.

"No, no I'm serious," the wealthy uncle said. "I'll get you anything you want. You know I can afford it."

"OK" Jim replied, "I want the same kind of car you have—a red Jaguar sports car."

Uncle Paul put out his right hand and said, "Shake on it. You graduate from college in four years with highest honors and on the day of your graduation, a brand new red Jaguar sports car will be sitting right there in your driveway. But there's one stipulation—you can't tell anyone about our deal until after you graduate."

As soon as school started in September, Jim became a real student. He had never done that before. Every time he felt like sleeping late-he got up early. Every time he felt like cutting class-he went to class. Every time he felt like hanging out with his friends-he went to the library and studied.

To make a long story short, he graduated summa cum laude just like his uncle. And as his uncle predicted, the night he graduated, his parents had another party for him.

A lot of his friends, neighbors and relatives were there again. However, one relative was missing—Uncle Paul. Jim felt betrayed, but he kept checking the driveway for his car anyway. All the guests left by 11:30 p.m. and the family started cleaning up. When they were all done Mom said, "Everyone out by the garage. I want to take some family pictures." While everyone was posing, Mom hit the remote that was hidden in her pocket and the garage door went up.

And there it was —a brand-new, red Jaguar sports car.

Even though it was late, Jim drove over and picked up his best friend Ray. Ray was really into cars. He was in awe of Jim's new car. He took Jim to a drag strip-like straightway, where police never go so that they could see how fast the car could go. Jim got it up to 105 M.P.H.

Ray said, "You don't know how to drive a car like this. Let me show you."

He got behind the wheel, but couldn't do much better. A little embarrassed, he said, "This car should be able to go 170, there must be something wrong with it. You'd better take it back to the dealer tomorrow."

When Jim drove into the dealership the next day, he was greeted by the sales manager. When the sales manager heard the problem, he brought in the master mechanic. The mechanic put the Jaguar up on the lift. He looked at the car for about a minute, then brought it down, turned to Jim and said, "You're the kid who got all A's in college, aren't you?"

Jim nodded.

"How long have you been driving?"

"Four years."

"Let's see if I got this right. You've been driving for four years and you're smart enough to get all A's in college, but you don't know that you don't drive a $75,000 sports car with the emergency brake on!"

Here's the big question: Do you have your emergency brake on while you are playing golf?

You probably don't even realize that you have an emergency brake.

You do.

Let me prove how destructive your mental emergency brake can be…

*Do you ever perform better in practice than while on the course?*
Blame it on your mental emergency brake.

*Do you ever get intimidated by another golfer and play terribly?*
Blame it on your mental emergency brake.

*Do you ever lose to someone you've easily beaten before?*
You know why - because you have your mental emergency brake on.

---

Look at all the thousands of hours you've spent hitting balls on the range, spending money on lessons, and putting on the practice green. In just a few seconds, this mental emergency brake can destroy all your preparation.

Don't worry. I'm going to spend the rest of this book giving you techniques to learn how to release your mental emergency brake so you can unleash your true potential to play and perform at a higher level than you ever have before.

Right now, you might be asking why you haven't released this mental emergency brake before.

There is a simple answer. You never know it existed.

It's impossible to control something that you didn't even know about. Now that you know about it, you'll learn how you can control it. Once you learn how to release your emergency brake, you'll be able to go all out without holding back.

As a golfer, do you feel you have to play a great round? Do you focus entirely on your score, moment by moment. How many times do you have a solid front nine and then all you can think about is what you have to shoot on the back nine to break your lowest score?

So how are you going to make sure your mental emergency brake is released? You only have to do two simple things.

## Part 1—How to Release Your Mental Emergency Break

Your emergency brake is on if you feel that you must play great golf or if you feel you have to win or beat your opponents. It's on big time! Golfers or athletes of any sport don't perform well under this type of pressure.

There is a simple solution to this problem. If you want to win and you don't feel you have to win, you'll release your mental emergency break immediately.

One of the secrets to releasing your mental emergency break is to follow this advice before you play your next round.

If you want to lower your score tomorrow, read this book tonight.

Look at the third word in the preceding phrase. It's "want."

When you think to yourself, "I have to win" and "I must win," it creates tension. When you think, "I want to win," it reduces tension.

"I have to win" and "I must win" cause you to over react. "I want to win" will help you under react.

The change you can make right now is to go from thinking…

I "have to" win tomorrow to I "want to" win tomorrow.

I "must win" tomorrow to I "want to" win tomorrow.

If you feel that you have to win or play your very best during your next round, you're harming your game by putting too much pressure on yourself.

Suppose you hold a hose and try to water your lawn. But you are doing one thing wrong – you are standing on the hose.

*What will happen?* The pressure in the hose will build up until it explodes!

That's what happens when you feel you must win or you feel you have to win - you put too much pressure on yourself and you'll feel like your going to explode. Step off the hose.

Many years ago, I worked with a top high school golfer. Well, she was one of the top golfers until her senior year in high school. Her senior year started as a disaster. She was performing worse than she did her freshman year.

We finally figured out what the problem was. Before each round her senior year, her coach and parents would point out to her which college coaches were at tournaments scouting her. Her parents and her coaches created this "I have to win/I must win" mindset. This was putting too much pressure on her. She felt she had to impress the college coaches so that they would offer her a scholarship. This was a losing mindset.

There is a happy ending however. This young golfer had a discussion with a wrestler from her school who got her back to competing like her "old self."

This young man performed great as a junior. However, during his senior year in high school, everything changed. Wrestlers that he used to beat easily were now beating him. Tournaments he used to win, he wasn't even making it to the finals.

Needless to say, he was very stressed. This was his senior year. Everyone thought this was his year to win the state championship. Everyone expected him to get a full scholarship to one of the big wrestling schools.

He consulted with a sport psychologist and told him all about the pressure he was under - wrestling, colleges, his parents and his girlfriend. The sport psychologist taught the wrestler a simple relaxation technique. The wrestler did this exercise every single night and he felt better <u>almost instantly</u>.

Within a week he was his "old self" again. Within two weeks, he was wrestling better than ever before. His coach was amazed with this dramatic turn-around. The coach wanted to know what happened.

"Well, I went to see that sport psychologist you told me about. He taught me a very simple relaxation technique that I do every night."

"Can you tell me how to do it?" asked the coach.

"Sure," the wrestler said. "Every night before I go to sleep, I sit in a chair and close my eyes for about twenty minutes and I repeat a phrase over and over again to myself."

"Would you be betraying a trust if you told me what the phrase was?" the coach wondered.

"No, not at all. I just sit in a chair, relax, close my eyes and repeat to myself over and over again, 'I don't give a damn. I don't give a damn. I don't give a damn.'"

It wasn't that the wrestler didn't give a damn about how he was wrestling. It was that he didn't give a damn about what everyone was going to think and what everyone was going to say about him.

The golfer told me that this story helped her before competitions. Rather than thinking about what the college coaches were thinking, she started thinking, "I don't give a damn."

Maybe you might even want to try this technique. Here's how you can lessen the pressure on yourself right now...

Rule #1. Realize there are no "must-win" rounds or holes of golf.

If you're dreading tomorrow, it's probably because you feel you must win or perform well enough to impress the other golfers you will play with.

Rule #2. There are no "must make" putts.

When you feel you must win or you have to make a putt – you are weak.

When you want to win – you are strong.

"Musts" and "have to's" create stress. "Want to's" create energy!

When you feel you want to win, then you're psychologically in great shape! You're not putting too much pressure on yourself.

**Part 2—How to Release Your Mental Emergency Brake**

Your emergency brake is on when your focus is on winning.

Your emergency brake is off when you focus on giving your best effort each shot or putt.

Let's briefly talk about mental focus here (we'll go into greater detail in future chapters)

Most golfers focus on the wrong thing - they focus on beating the guys they are playing with that round.

Let me see if I can get you to focus on the wrong thing. Here is a short riddle.

Anna's mother has three daughters. One is named Penny; another is named Nickel. What is the name of her third daughter?

Do you think the answer is Dime, Quarter or Half-Dollar? That's because you're focusing on the wrong side of the riddle.

If you focus on the first two words of the riddle, "Anna's mother," you realize that the third daughter's name is Anna!

Most golfer's do the same thing. They're focusing on the wrong thing. They're focused on beating their fellow golfers. This is a big mistake.

Why? Because you don't have any control over your opponents. But, you do have control over your effort.

Gandhi once said, "Full effort is full victory."

Here is one of the key concepts I want you to take away from this book: **focus on execution, not outcome.**

Dr. Alan Goldberg is one of the top sports psychologists in the country. In fact, we'll be reading some of his training tips later in this book. In his seminars, he tells the story of when he was a freshman at the University of Massachusetts. He played #1 singles on the tennis team. At the end of the season, he was playing in the finals for the Yankee Conference Championship. This is a big deal for a freshman.

Alan easily won the first set 6-3. He was ahead 5-2 in the second set and was serving for the match. In other words, he needed only four more points to win the Yankee Conference title.

When changing sides between games, Alan got a glimpse of the trophy table and he saw the big trophy that the champion would receive.

Four points away from winning, Alan says that he started thinking about the trophy. He started thinking how cool it would be to bring the trophy back to his dorm.

All of the sudden, he started focusing more on the prize and less on the next point.

He started focusing more on the outcome and less on the effort.

Alan lost the next two sets.

The moral of the story is: You can't keep one eye on winning and the other eye on the ball. It won't work.

This same mental lapse even impacts pro golfers who start thinking about their victory speeches before they play the 18th hole. This might be what happened to Phil Mickelson who had the win in hand at the 2006 U.S. Open, only to collapse at the very end with a horrible drive on the final hole.

After a loss, a frustrated Vince Lombadi reportedly said, "We lost because we were focused on winning while they were focused on football."

Keep your focus on the process – not on the finished results. **Golfers are notorious for having a great front 9 and thinking what they need to shoot to break their all time best score. At that moment, they have doomed themselves in most cases**. They have taken their focus from where it should be – the next drive - and replaced it by thinking about breaking their lowest score.

**GREAT GOLF Tip** ③

**Conquer Irrational Expectations to Avoid Choking**

Every golfer instinctively knows how damaging negative thoughts are to performance. But not so obvious is the damage caused by irrational thinking. Some typical examples include: "To be a success, I must never make the same mistake twice."; "Winners never fail when the pressure is on."; "Choking is a sign of weakness and can't be tolerated."

This constitutes irrational thinking. Research shows that many of the performance problems golfers struggle with originate from this type of thinking. We often find that negative attitudes stem directly from irrational ones. Once an irrational attitude takes root, you are destined for trouble.

The most common problems center around attitudes toward mistakes and self-control during a round. For many golfers the management of mistakes represents a major roadblock between themselves and the realization of their goals. Irrational thoughts place you in "no-win" situations.

Here are some practical tips to keep irrational thinking from getting the better of you the next time out on the course:
    1. Understand that mistakes are a part of learning and becoming a better golfer.
    2. Mistakes represent feedback. They point you in a direction to adjust your game so you will not keep repeating the same mistake. Without mistakes, no learning or improvement will occur.
    3. Patience and persistence produce positive performance. Without self-control, you become a pawn of fate and circumstance. Poor self-control can cause performance blocks and lessen the ability to learn.

To avoid this, remember:
    1. Even the best golfers in the world choke sometimes. "Choking" can be an indication that great effort is being put forth.
    2. The more "choking" is feared; the more likely it will occur.
    3. Luck or fate rarely determines the outcome of a contest.

With the hyper competitive culture in which we live, golfers can develop an obsession with winning that is clearly self-defeating.

To alter this obsession, try the following: A. To change irrational attitudes, identify which beliefs and attitudes are truly irrational and interfering with your golf game. B. Make winning your next round a goal - not the goal. C. Focus should be on performance and how well you play that day, not winning.

" I have lost tournaments by trying too hard."

— Davis Love III

"How to Succeed: Try hard enough.
How to Fail: Try too hard."

— Malcom Forbes, Publisher

"I don't know if I'll ever win it again.
Frankly, I don't really care."

— Jack Nicklaus,
after winning his 6th Masters Tournament

## THE KILLER ATTITUDE THAT SPOILS YOUR GREAT ROUND

Let's review what we have learned so far:

1. Do not feel that you must win.

2. Do feel that you want to win.

3. Do not focus on beating your opponent.

4. Focus on the execution not the outcome.

5. Focus on the process not the product (or end result).

I have a question to ask you. Why does it hurt so much when you lose or play poorly?

Answer: Because you care.

Caring is a good thing.

In order to be a great golfer, you have to care.

You've got to care to practice so much.

You've got to care to take lessons.

You've got to care to commit yourself to being a better golfer.

But, why are you so worried? Why are you so scared? Why do you feel you must win? Why do you feel you have to win? Why do you focus so much on winning and beating your fellow golfers?

I'll give you the answer: you care too much.

Caring is important. However, caring too much is destructive.

Herb Cohen is one of the world's top business negotiators. One of his books is titled:
'Negotiate this! By Caring, but Not T-H-A-T Much'

Cohen's point is that if you want to be a better negotiator, you can't care t-h-a-t much.

If you want to be a better golfer, you can't care t-h-a-t much.

When you care too much—you're weak.

When you care, but not too much- you're powerful!

In the movie "The Fan," there's a scene that's a perfect example of this.

Robert De Niro plays an obsessive baseball fan who asks his hero, slugger Bobby Rayburn (played by Wesley Snipes), how he broke out of his hitting slump. "I just stopped caring," the ball player said. "I stopped caring, I relaxed and then I started hitting."

---

Let's look at this another way. Think of two people you know who are dating. In any romantic relationship, one person usually cares more about the relationship than the other person. Let me ask you this: Who controls the relationship, the person who cares more or the person who cares less? It's always the person who cares less. There's power in caring less whether you're talking about romance or sports.

Once you start caring too much, you start being too careful.

When you're too careful, the following things happen:

- You start thinking too much.
- You start worrying too much.
- You start being too scared.
- You make the competition too special.
- You focus too much on winning the round.

Then what happens? You don't play up to your potential.

It's OK to care. Just don't care too much. Tomorrow's round of golf is important. You may be playing in the club championship or trying to break in to PGA qualifying school.

When you care too much, you make tomorrow special. When you make any one event special, you will ramp up the pressure on yourself.

---

Every time you practice, every round you play, every time you do anything with your golf game - it's important. But it's not special. Golfers at any level do not perform well when they think something is "special." I'd give you the same advice even if you were playing in the Super Bowl tomorrow. Don't treat the Super Bowl like the Super Bowl. Act as if it were like any other game. Don't make it special.

If you want to make it special, just use these 14 killer words that are almost sure to destroy a great round:

- "This is it."
- "It's now or never."
- "It's do or die."
- "There's no tomorrow."

These words make something special, when it's only important. When golfers make something special, they perform worse.

Every time you play a round of golf - it's important, not special.

Start thinking this way. It's the way a winner thinks!

There's a country song that makes this point perfectly. In "Come from the Heart," Kathy Mattea sings…

"You have to sing like you don't need the money. You have to love like you will never get hurt. You have to dance like nobody's watching. You have to come from the heart, if you want it to work."

# GREAT GOLF Tip 4

**Stop Performance Killing Thoughts**

In his book *Sports Slumpbusting*, Sports Psychologist Dr. Alan Goldberg lists a 5-step strategy to counter "performance thought killers".

Let's say you just missed an easy putt late in your round. You may start to think: "I can't believe I missed that shot. What a choke! Why can't I ever come through in the clutch?!"

If you stay with this kind of internal punishment, you'll be too nervous, distracted, and unsure of yourself to play well. In the few minutes that remain before the next hole, your use of the thought-stopping technique might resemble the following:

**Stage 1)** Recognize that you are emotionally pounding on yourself.
**Stage 2)** Think to yourself: "Whoa! Stop!"
**Stage 3)** Take a few slow, deep breathes, imagining you can breathe away all that mental garbage.
**Stage 4)** Deliberately turn the negative chatter to positive by thinking, "You've played a great round so far. Forget it...let it go...get back to thinking about the next shot."
**Stage 5)** Finally, as you walk out on to the next tee box, put your focus of concentration on executing a well placed drive in the center of the fairway.

You can use a number of streamlined variations of thought stopping in practice or during competition. Consider the following strategies:

**The Rubber Band** - Put an elastic band on your wrist, and every time you become aware of a negative thought, snap the band against your wrist. The sudden quick pain will "snap you out" of the negativity and remind you to get your focus back on track.

**Exhale** - Imagine that you have a pipe-like connection between your brain and lungs. Just by exhaling, you can eliminate any negative self-talk that arises, as if your exhalation were an exhaust pipe. You can inhale relaxation and calming thoughts and exhale negativity.

**Erase it** - Imagine that you can take the negative self-talk and write it on a piece of paper or a chalkboard. Take an eraser and rub out the negative writing until it disappears completely from your mind's eye.

**Change the Channel** - Imagine that you can create an image of the negative self-talk as if it were on a TV screen. Change the channel or otherwise blur the screen so that the picture with the writing becomes unreadable.

> "Golf is a lot like a love affair. If you don't take it seriously, it's no fun. If you take it too seriously, it breaks your heart."
> — Arnold Daley, Sports Writer

> "The game has to be fun if you are going to be any good at all."
> — Don Zimmer, Pro Baseball Manager

## THE ONE OVERLOOKED KEY TO SHOOTING A LOWER SCORE

I know something about you – you're a golfer who is motivated to improve his or her game. Why else would you be reading this book?

I know something else about you – sometimes you get too motivated, like before a big tournament at your club. This is not good.

A lot of people believe… if some is good, more is better.

This is dangerous thinking.

Let me give you a ridiculous example. Suppose you have a headache, and you take two aspirin and you get rid of your headache in 20 minutes. Would you take 20 aspirin to get rid of the headache in two minutes? Of course you wouldn't. Because you know… if some is good, more is not necessarily better.

Being motivated is good, but being too motivated is bad. Caring is good, but caring too much is bad. Making tomorrow's round important is good, but making it too important is bad.

Here's what I want you to remember…sometimes less is more.

Less tension will allow you to be more intense. The next time you are getting ready to tee it up I want you to…be intense without being tense.

Loosen up. Go all out. Have fun. Play with vigor and reckless abandon (that's attitude I'm talking about – not poor shot planning, which I'll address in a future chapter).

It's amazing that you will perform so well when you simply…let loose and have some fun.

There is a great scene in the movie Stroke of Genius where golfing legend Bobby Jones is playing in a major charity event early on in his career.

He hits a poor shot and has a temper tantrum meltdown where he throws his club.

Frustrated, he tells his playing partner, "I haven't done anything yet. I'm just an amateur champion."

His partner's reply is advice all golfers could learn from: "You will do great things – as soon as you learn to get out of your own way."

This is the one overlooked key to playing your best golf. Learn to loosen up and get out of your own way.

Let me tell you the secret of a great athlete…

Willie Stargell, the legendary Pittsburgh Pirate baseball player was once asked to share the secret of his success. Stargell said that he just followed the advice the umpire gives after the National Anthem is played.

After the National Anthem, the umpire yells, "Play ball."

Stargell said: "I don't work ball. I play ball. I never go to the ball park to work. I always go to play."

There are three types of golfers: Pretenders, Performers, and Players.

Pretenders show up physically. They compete with their bodies.

Performers are a step above pretenders. They compete with their bodies and their minds.

But Players have put it all together. They compete physically, mentally and emotionally. They've released their emergency brakes so that they are...1) Physically intense. 2) Have the "Eye of the Tiger" Mental Focus. 3) Are emotionally energized. Pretenders and Performers can't compete with Players.

All golfers are different. But if you can adapt the preceding mental skills to fit your personality, you will be able to fight through any adverse situation by being mentally tough.

In his book *The New Toughness Training for Sports*, author James Loehr writes that mentally tough athletes combat negative thoughts, and can even change the way they are feeling.

Tough competitors consistently use images of success of fighting back, of having fun, of staying relaxed, of being strong in the face of adversity, to move their chemistry in those directions. Loehr believes that golfers who want to develop mental toughness should practice daily to make their self-image "strong, vivid, and courageous."

Mentally tough golfers learn to see stress as a challenge, not a threat. Did you know that golfers who view stressful situations as a threat actually produce hormones and chemicals in their body that can impair physical and mental performance?

Golfers who meet stress as a challenge create a rush of adrenaline and sugar inside their bodies - a natural "high" that is probably responsible for what is typically referred to as a sense of "flow," or heightened awareness as they perform. If you can learn to encounter stress and say, "Great!" I'm ready for this!" you are more likely to recover from a poor shot quickly.

On the other hand, a problem that can plague more elite golfers who get in a rhythm of playing really well is that they will sometimes start hitting the ball 10 to 20 yards past their target because they fail to deal with the adrenaline. So it's crucial to monitor your own level of anxiety and adrenaline. (We'll go into more detail later.)

Mentally tough golfers use humor to break up tension. When one thinks nutty, goofy, silly, funny, off-the-wall thoughts, fear and anger vaporize.

Mentally tough golfers know how to learn and move on quickly from mistakes. Sports psychologists say the ability to ask tough questions ("What could I have done differently?" or "What have I learned that I can use in the future?") is critical.

Mentally tough golfers have a "just for today" spirit. Successful golfers develop the self-discipline to commit themselves to doing it right "just for today."

Mentally, it's easier to think about controlling what you do on a single day, then getting overwhelmed by thinking of the bigger picture of what you want to accomplish over the long run.

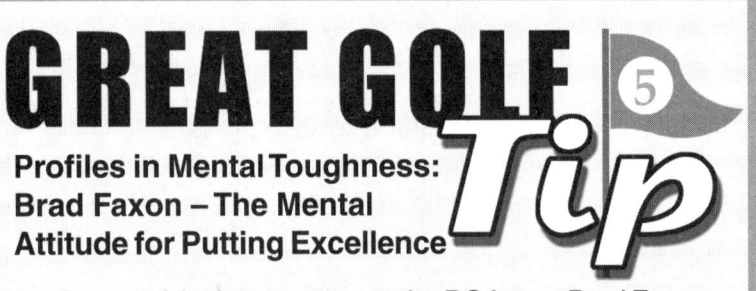

**GREAT GOLF Tip 5**

**Profiles in Mental Toughness: Brad Faxon – The Mental Attitude for Putting Excellence**

As one of the best putters on the PGA tour, Brad Faxon has a success formula that has served him well. He has led the tour in putting average, 3 out of the past 6 years.

**Step 1)** "Don't be afraid to miss. It's the fear factor. Worrying gets you into trouble and ties you up in knots. You develop the yips by being afraid of missing. Don't think too much about it. Look at the line and trust your first instinct. You can't be a good putter with too much conscious thought."

**Step 2)** "You need a good stroke and a good attitude. Attitude is the most important. If I'm not in the right frame of mind, I don't putt well."

**Step 3)** "You need a consistent physical routine. That makes you more confident. I prefer if my body moves a little bit. Staying perfectly still cripples me."

**Step 4)** "Like any other sport, being great requires practice and believing in yourself. I wasn't always a good putter. When I practice, I think about what it takes to become a great putter. It frustrates me when people say I'm a natural and don't have to practice."

Here are some specific examples of Faxon's success formula:

- "Before I start a round, I take a pen and draw a line on the ball about an inch and a half long. That line faces the direction I'm going to putt. I put the ball down with the line pointing toward the highest point in the break."

- "On every green, I check out the wind, the break, whether the putt is uphill or downhill, and if the green is firm or soft. I don't take a lot of time doing all that. I pick out a line and know where I am going to aim."

- "I take a final look from behind the ball. I step up and visualize the putt and get set. I square the putter to the ball at address. Sometimes I take a practice stroke. Other times, not. I look at the hole once, then twice. Once I look back at the ball the second time, the shot starts. I don't allow anything to creep into my head."

- "The toe of the putter is open a little coming back. It closes, then opens a little bit on follow through. The toe flows. That's why I prefer a heel-shafted putter. The stroke should be the same every time you putt. The longer the putt, the longer the stroke."

The legendary Ben Hogan once stood over a crucial putt. Suddenly, a loud train whistle blared off in the distance. After sinking the putt, Hogan was asked if the whistle bothered him.

"What whistle?," Hogan replied.

"It's nothing new or original to say that golf is played one stroke at a time. But it took me many years to realize it."
— Bobby Jones

"I didn't win in the 1930s because I hadn't yet learned to concentrate - to ignore the gallery and the other golfers and to shut my mind against everything but my own game."
— Ben Hogan

## Chapter Six

**PROVEN CONCENTRATION TECHNIQUES TO ACHIEVE THE FOCUS OF CHAMPIONS**

Allow me to switch gears a bit and put on my teaching hat to help you obtain absolute mental focus. For the next four chapters, I'm going to go into greater detail on how to take your golf game to new heights. The first five chapters discussed various mental attitude principles you can put to use immediately. These next four chapters are sport psychology techniques you can work on perfecting for the rest of your golfing life.

First, let's start with the simple concept of routines. These can be used before a competition (often referred to as pre-performance rituals) and during a competition to establish a set pattern to approach and execute each shot.

A routine is something that an athlete always does the same way. Pre competition rituals help narrow focus at the very start of the event. An example is always wearing the same shirt every time you play a competitive round. Tiger Woods likes to wear a red shirt during the final round of every tournament he plays. Bobby Jones would always touch his lucky pendant before teeing off on the first hole.

Most athletes have pre-game routines. You look at a baseball player like Wade Boggs. He had every minute of his game day programmed down to what he would eat, the exact time he would wake and what type of under garments he would wear, followed by exactly how his pre-game batting and fielding practice would be executed. You will see other baseball players adjust their glove a certain way as they step outside the batters box between pitches.

You can watch basketball players as they bounce the ball a certain amount of times before taking a free throw or a field goal kicker who will swing his leg 4 times before lining up to attempt a kick.

First and foremost, routines give athletes a sense of control. For example, a baseball pitcher has no control over how tight the umpire calls the strike zone, the weather, the talent level of the opposition, or the crowd. So the routine of towing the rubber, scuffing the ball, punching his mitt two of three times before throwing the pitch – all of that gives him a sense of control and it eases him into the game. The routine provides relaxation in a moment of stress.

If you are someone who likes to talk a lot on the course, you can use a technique that worked well for Lee Trevino. Before he would stand over the ball, he would stop talking and tear the Velcro on and off his glove. That was his signal to get his focus where it needed to be – in the present moment ready to swing.

---

For golfers, the development of a structured pre and post-shot routine is critical to your success on the course. A routine provides you with an organized means of controlling concentration and intensity. You can systematically and effectively address all key elements of pre and post shot preparation. Let's examine in detail how this can work for you.

First, during the time between shots, prior to beginning the routine, you should "turn off" your focus and intensity. While walking or riding toward the next shot, you should engage in tasks of your choosing that allow you to forget about your previous and upcoming shots, and, more generally, the competitive pressure of the round. Useful activities to release focus and intensity include talking with playing partners about non golf topics, listening to music on a portable stereo, and enjoying the weather and the scenic views around you.

Second, you need to assess the shot situation, including lie, distance, target, wind, and club selection.

Third, try to monitor your intensity level, to determine your present state relative to your ideal condition. Take a few deep breaths before taking a practice swing. To this point in the pre-shot routine, all preparation is done from behind the ball. All subsequent steps in the routine, which involve "grooving" the shot itself, are accomplished standing over the ball.

Fourth, you should rehearse the upcoming shot using imagery or key words with an emphasis on feeling the proper execution. Most golfers like to use key words, or "swing thoughts," to remind them of a critical part of their technique. "Strike", "Power", "Groove", "Smooth" are all examples. You can find the best key word that works for you. Repeat the key word to ingrain the proper technique with your practice swing.

Fifth, rehearse the actual swing several times. Find a number you are comfortable with and try to stick to it.

Sixth, immediately execute the shot while your mental motor is primed for correct execution. You should no longer be thinking about the shot, simply execute.

It is often thought that the routine ends after the ball is struck. However, a brief post shot routine will further enhance performance. First, you may use a technique called "replay or edit." This involves using imagery or other forms of mental rehearsal following either a good or poor shot. If you hit a good shot, the most important thing you want to do is remember it, so you can "replay" it several times to ingrain its image and feeling.

If you hit a poor shot, the last thing you want to do is remember it, so you need to "edit" it several times — mentally rehearsing the shot correctly. This way you will "cleanse" the poor image, thought, and feeling, and ingrain a correct image, thought, and feeling.

(These routines must part be of your practice preparation as well which we'll go into greater detail in the next chapter)

---

### Find Your "Focus Point" to Achieve Absolute Concentration

Once you have your pre and post shot routine down, the next area you can work on is concentration. Make no mistake —concentration is a skill that can be enhanced through practice and mental discipline.

Concentration is being aware of only the present—not the future or the past.

You must find a "focus point" as your center of concentration. For most golfers, that little white ball must be at the center of your attention.

The key is to let your mind remain focused on that object (the golf ball) to the complete exclusion of all outside stimuli and thoughts. A player's subconscious mind knows how to perform the stroke. The key then becomes trusting one's own ability to execute the shot.

You have to be in a state of relaxed concentration —to let the body perform naturally.

When concentrating, a player's complete conscious mental attention should be on the successful completion of the shot or stroke to be performed and should remain focused on that skill until it is completed. You must have only a positive mental picture in your mind of successfully performing your next shot.

If any negative feelings or thoughts enter the mind while performing, even for a split second, you will break your concentration and possibly flub the shot.

While performing in a competitive situation, your focus of concentration should be totally on the ball and the skill you are about to perform, whether it's a six foot putt or a tee shot. The mind should be perfectly clear.

If you develop total concentration while performing, the mind will become "one" with your performance. You will not be influenced by outside stimuli. They will have no sense of time. You will not feel any emotion about performance since you will be experiencing total involvement with what you are doing.

This is the state that golfers experience when they say they have played "out of their mind." They were able to experience the ultimate high of concentration while they were performing. Their conscious self-ego is able to completely let go and let their subconscious computer take over and control their performance.

Fear will never enter the mind of the golfer who has mastered concentration skills.

When you allow the emotion of fear to enter and control your conscious mind, you start to think about losing or hitting the ball poorly or a number of other self-defeating thoughts. When you begin to lose your self-control over the conscious power of concentration and let fear "hang a noose around your neck," you increase the odds of performing poorly.

One of the keys to make sure you will be able to concentrate the next time you play golf is to set limits on yourself and others both before and during competition periods. Setting limits is something only you can do. You must assume personal responsibility to ensure that these limits are respected.

For example, only you can ensure a good night's rest before the event. The day of an event is not a good time to have your first bowl of "five alarm" chili. Eat light—just enough so you don't get hunger pains on the course.

The night before or day of competition is also not the best time to have a serious conversation with your significant other about your relationship. Think through what you need to do to compete your best and make sure that you follow through.

## Breathing Regulation and Simulation Training

Deep breathing is one of the best methods ever developed for self control. If your breathing starts to get short and shallow, you are under stress and about to lose concentration. Slow, deep breaths will help you maintain control over your emotions.

Tom Watson, winner of 8 major championships, was one of the best golfers at using this deep breathing technique to relax himself. He would always self-monitor his breathing to keep himself in the right frame of mind. The ability to control your breathing is essential. Knowing how you are breathing and regulating it will make a huge impact on how well you are able to concentrate and stay absolutely focused.

Stay in the present moment where the action currently is. If you are thinking about an error that happened a moment ago and worrying that it might happen again, you are not in the present, which destroys your concentration. Deep breathing can also help you stay in the present moment.

I recommend the use of simulation training. This means making some of your practice sessions as you approach the event as much like actual competition conditions as possible. This will help you feel more prepared and comfortable when the actual event day arrives. Simulation training also allows you to check to see if your pre and post shot routine is effective or needs to be tweaked.

What will you do to handle the bad breaks you will inevitably face during your next round of golf? You need to expect the unexpected to happen and prepare for it. Nothing can break concentration faster than an unexpected happening for which you feel unprepared. Let's say you hit the perfect five iron to a par three that is headed dead center of the green, when all the sudden a burst of wind kicks your shot far in the rough.

Think through all the things that can go wrong and plan a possible response. For example, you will want to think ahead about how to handle an extremely windy day. Nothing can frustrate golfers more than having to adjust their games to windy conditions. (We'll address this in greater detail in the next chapter on practice).

There are many things beyond our control during a round of golf, but two things we can control are our preparation and response to poor shots.

Remember to have as much fun as possible. No one exhibits a higher level of concentration than children at play. Enjoy competing as much as you can and that will naturally boost your ability to concentrate on the task at hand.

---

**3 Simple Concentration Exercises**

Finally, I want to offer three simple exercises to improve concentration. While performing these exercises, be aware of when your focus of concentration is interrupted. When this happens, don't get upset or angry. Simply breathe deeply, relax, and let your mind return to your focus of concentration. These exercises may not produce overnight results but will sharpen the mind over time.

1. Count from one to one hundred. Mentally picture each number as you say it. Progress to counting to five hundred.

2. Hold a golf ball in your hand. Find a distinguishing feature on the ball as you concentrate, such as a letter in the name on the ball, a dimple, etc. Try to concentrate on this feature on the ball for one minute. Add minutes as you feel ready and make sure you don't break your concentration. If you do, go back and start the exercise again.

3. Find a distinguishing feature of some object in a room at home. Try to concentrate on this feature for one minute, blocking out all peripheral stimuli. Progress at your own pace to five minutes.

## GREAT GOLF Tip 6
**Power Words Improve Concentration**

While playing a round, golfers tend to think about too many things: what happened two minutes ago, what may happen in the next two minutes, or what they are going to drink at the 19$^{th}$ hole, etc. The human mind is capable of processing thousands of thoughts at the same time. The best athletes in the world are able to focus their thoughts only on what is happening in the present and what they have to do to accomplish their goals.

Two techniques that superstar athletes use to keep thoughts focused on the "here and now" are the very same ones that can help your golf game as well.

The first is a single word or mantra that athletes repeat over and over mentally and verbally. One of the best words for golfers to use is simply "Ball".

"Power", "Impact", and "Now" are other great one word key words to sharpen concentration. This will block out distractions and wandering thoughts. When you feel concentration starting to wander, you can repeat the word to yourself to snap back into focus.

The second technique is a visual "mantra" to focus eyesight on, which in turn focuses the mind.

When baseball's all time hit leader Pete Rose stepped up to the plate, he always kept his eye focused on the pitcher's hand. His key word to concentrate was to think "base hit".

You may want to look out and pick a visual marker near the intended target and think to yourself "Strike" or "Target" to remind you to concentrate just before executing a swing.

Warning: If you are playing a round with a gallery watching, keep your head looking straight ahead the majority of the time. Jack Nicklaus was considered aloof for much of his career because he rarely acknowledged the gallery. His mind was always focused on what he had to accomplish.

Crowds can easily take your mind off playing your best round. Whether you try to impress the crowd, or simply the other guys in your foursome, instead of focusing on the task at hand, your performance will suffer.

"All my life I've tried to hit practice shots with great care. I try to have a clear cut purpose in mind for every swing. I always practiced as I intended to play. I learned a long time ago there is a limit on the number of shots you can hit effectively before you start to lose concentration on your basic objectives."

— Jack Nicklaus

"I hated playing in the rain and cold, but my opponents had to play under the same conditions. I was more composed and better able to emotionally handle the effects of the weather than they were. I never wanted to turn the weather into a excuse. I practiced under the conditions that I would play under."

— Arnold Palmer

## PRACTICE HABITS TO REVOLUTIONIZE THE WAY YOU PLAY THE GAME

Getting better and lowering your score requires not only the right mental focus on the course, but on the practice range and putting green as well. You must decide to practice being a more mentally focused golfer before you can implement the techniques I've been talking about in this book.

The rest of this chapter is dedicated to helping you practice with the right mental focus. I'm going to share with you practice tips that will revolutionize the way you approach the game of golf. I've compiled some of the absolute best thinking on the subject of practice from the leading edge sports psychologists in the world.

Dr. Fran Pirozzolo consults with some of the top touring professionals. As part of his consulting work, Dr. Pirozzolo insists that during the Wednesday practice round before an upcoming tournament that the golfer hit a terrible tee shot on purpose. The pro is instructed not to tell his caddy or his fellow golfers that the shot was made on purpose. The idea is to get the golfer used to the embarrassment of an inevitable poor shot during the tournament.

Dr. Pirozzolo will caddy with a professional himself and when things get too tense, he will try to get his client to relax by discussing football or the player's family so that the tournament is more like a practice round than an actual high stakes tournament.

He has discovered over the years that not very many athletes actually crave the make or break moments – whether it's taking the final shot in basketball, the late innings of a $7^{th}$ game series in baseball or battling for the lead in the U.S. Open in the Final Round. Most just want to get the competition over with.

To come through in the most pressure filled moments starts during the practice rounds, Dr. Pirozzolo asks golfers to envision themselves in the heat of the battle during the start of the tournament. 1998 U.S. Open champ Hank Kuehne now starts focusing on his Sunday performance during his daily practice sessions instead of getting ready just for the opening round on Thursday. You don't have to be in preparation for the U.S. Open to make the very same mental preparation work for you.

---

**Practice Preparation**

Dr. Ken Ravizza has worked with the Los Angeles Dodgers, New York Jets, and Gold Medal winning U.S. Olympic teams.

He feels the key to having good practice sessions is to "prepare to prepare." If you aren't retired, you most likely have limited time to practice so it becomes critical that you are present and really ready to go from the start of the time you visit the range.

One good rule of thumb is to have a practice schedule mapped out in advance so you know what you plan to work on for that hour or two.

Penn State football coach Joe Paterno has a blue line that goes all around the practice field. When the athlete steps over that line, they are symbolically making a commitment to that day's practice. A golfer can do the same thing. Once they pull the clubs out of the car, that's their ticket to forget about anything else on their mind and focus solely on getting better at their golf game.

You can have a "thought for the day" that the practice tries to capture. This will help you get more focused on what you want to accomplish at that day's practice. For example, you can say to yourself as you warm up, "Today, I will concentrate on making every shot target oriented. I will not hit a shot today without having a target and distance in mind." That is something you should always try to do by the way.

Here is another "thought of the day" example: "Today I want to work on recovering from poor shots. After each poor shot I hit today, I will practice how I will respond as if I'm on the course working through the very same problem."

According to Dr. Ravizza even getting started the right way is critical to having a good practice session: "If the golfer isn't ready to go, they can check themselves. If they aren't at green light, don't go to the range. Take some time to release your emotions. Find a place to unwind for a few minutes before getting started."

And if you get off to a really poor start with your practice, he offers further advice:

"Some teams I have worked with have what's called a "zero station." Here, if you are having a really poor practice, you can take yourself out of the action and sit down for a few minutes and re-group without any pressure. It's a wonderful technique that golfers can take advantage of as well because it validates and reminds them to be aware of their own performance. It's key to be able to self-identify problems as they occur. When they learn to see and feel when their performance is starting to slip, they have taken the first step to correct the problem."

Ravizza asks athletes whom he consults with to break down their game into 3 areas of their own awareness of what is happening to them mentally. He uses the analogy of a red, green or yellow light for athletes to determine where they are emotionally. Golf is a game where it is vital to live in the moment. If you are not aware that you are in a bad place mentally or emotionally, it will cause you to make bad decisions on the course.

Typically, a golfer will have three types of inner dialogue. With green light, you feel good, you are in the present moment and thinking about what you are supposed to do right now. Examples of green light thinking would be: "I'm ready. I'm good." You step in the tee box and think of nothing but being ready to hit the ball.

Yellow light (or warning signs) would be demonstrated by thoughts like, "My club feels heavy" or "I'm not seeing where the ball needs to go" or "I'm not sure how I should play this next shot."

Other examples include future thinking and looking ahead. This is exhibited by thoughts like: "I'm anxious about not shanking that next drive." Another common problem is past thinking and looking back: "I hope I don't 3 putt again."

Red light would be demonstrated by thoughts like "What am I doing here?" or "I'm never going to be able to hit it straight again." It's panic or 911 mode.

The key is being able to take a self-inventory, then learning how to correct yourself by having the right self-dialogue and right plan. (See tips section after chapter 4 about negative thought stopping).

## Dealing with Distractions

Distractions are a common cause of performance lags. They can come in all shapes and forms. It can be a comment made by a playing partner, weather conditions, or how we talk to ourselves. In any event, distractions can create inconsistencies in performances and keep us from achieving at the level that we are capable. All athletes seek that "can't miss" feeling.

Some golfers complain that they can't play well in damp or rainy conditions. Obviously, this approach to the game will cause performance to suffer. Taking the focus away from weather conditions and back to the essentials of the game will allow you to divert yourself from the distractions that get in the way of a great round.

During rainy conditions, many golfers tend to become more hurried and confused. They fail to account for the needed changes in their game consistent with the weather conditions. This can cause variations in performance, followed by enormous frustration. When you focus more on your intended target and swinging the same way you would in good weather, you will gain more confidence and become less preoccupied with the weather.

Practice is the best time to help identify various distracters to your golf game. This is the first step toward improvement. Once problems are pinpointed, you develop greater confidence by focusing attention away from both external and internal distractions.

Sports psychologist and golf consultant Dr. Dennis Sprague offers these six suggestions to deal with competitive distractions during your practice sessions.

1. *If possible, practice frequently and keep sessions short.*
If you practice too long, your concentration span becomes shorter and you may become easily distracted and less alert.

2. *Practice in all weather conditions.* Tough it out and practice under adverse conditions. It will pay huge dividends later.

3. *Always practice with a purpose.* If you are not working on some specific area of improvement then you are not maximizing your practice time.

4. *Add variation to your practice routine.* At times, we all get into ruts with our practice routine. It can become so regimented and mechanical that any benefits fail to translate to the always unpredictable demands of golf. Work on different types of body movements and mechanics. By becoming more versatile, you will be less susceptible to distraction.

5. *Use positive self-talk.* Chastising yourself with negative statements about the last time you blew a 3 shot lead only interferes with your performance and becomes a distraction. According to research, such negative thoughts can divert your attention from your game for as long as 9 minutes every time you do it.

6. *Have a partner or professional play the role of distractor.* The late Earl Woods used the following drills to help Tiger block out distractions at critical moments. Just as Tiger would be in his back swing he would:

- Jingle loose change in his pocket.

- Drop a golf bag.

- Roll balls in his line of vision.

When you practice staying focused with various distractions, you will bring that ability with you to the course.

**Self Coaching to Improve Awareness**

Here is another brief technique that will forever alter the way you work toward improving your game. I call it "self-coaching."

You may or may not work with a professional coach, but either way you have to learn how to manage your own energy – both mental and physical – while you practice.

This process involves being a good emotional coach to one self, not a technical coach (which is what golf teachers are for). Self-coaching is important for the stability of your game and to trust in your own ability.

As performance decreases, the challenge to trust increases. Thus, good self-coaching provides a stabilizing effect on trust, even with swings in performance.

Developing self-coaching involves three steps: (a) recognizing self-coaching as a performance tool that requires practice; (b) practicing a self-coaching sequence that involves recognition of self-coaching statements (positive or negative), stopping ineffective self-coaching statements, and replacing these with effective ones; and (c) developing and making use of affirmation statements.

**Confidence = Composure Under Pressure.**

Confidence can be viewed as a product of your concentration and composure levels; as you increase confidence and become more focused on concentration, your confidence level becomes more stable.

Recognizing that confidence is a dynamic entity that can fluctuate in response to one's perception of any one event during a round of golf, you must (a) learn to manage the degree of fluctuation concerning your level of intensity, and (b) develop a reference point regarding an ideal emotional state prior to performance.

Managing emotional energy (arousal) springs from your ability to be an effective self-coach, following both mistakes and achievements. This is the ability to handle the adrenaline rush I first mentioned in Chapter 5.

For example, it is vital that you learn to manage negative energy after mistakes and to express positive energy after successful shots or putts.

During practice, make a list of situations in which you will have to deal with adversity during a round of golf. How would you handle the following?

- Your ball goes out of bounds on your first tee shot.

- You three putt the $17^{th}$ green which allows your fiercest rival to take the lead going into the final hole.

- You clunk a ball into the water hazard on the $10^{th}$ after playing an incredible front 9.

Practice how you would emotionally handle each of these by coming up with a 'problem execution plan.'

The purpose of the plan is to consistently put you in a state of mind that is most conducive to trusting performance at that moment – to forget about the past mistake. This is done by structuring a plan that quickly moves you from analysis to trust.

## 4 R's of Performance Cycles

Dr. Ravizza has helped thousands of athletes by coming up with a system called the 4 R's of Performance Cycles - *Recognition, Release, Refocus, and Ready.* You can use it to quickly recover from mistakes on the course as well.

First, you recognize the blown performance. That happens instantly. You can see where the shot went. We're talking about recognizing where you are emotionally after the poor shot has been hit. What happens to your body in terms of heart rate, blood pressure, or muscle tension? What happens in terms of your thoughts? Do you lose focus? Do you start doubting yourself? What happens to your behavior—do you slow down or speed up? These are all great questions to quickly recognize where you are emotionally.

Next, you have to release your emotions. How do you let go of the bad shot or putt that just happened? The release may be picking up another ball out of your bag, saying a favorite power word or phrase that gets you back on track, and putting the ball back in your pocket. You may want to grip your club very hard, squeeze and release to blow off some steam. The bad shot is over. Nothing can be done. Look at a spot on the horizon to get your mind ready to get back into action.

Now, ask yourself, what do I need to do right now? What's my plan? Once I have my plan, I need to commit to it. If I'm going to hit a 5 iron the next shot, I need to commit to using that club and then focus on the target.

Once I have my plan, it's time to get ready to hit the next shot. How do you know that you are ready to hit the next shot? Breathe. Inhale, exhale. It's called taking a few trusting breaths.

Now, I'm committed to the club I'm going to hit. Inhale, exhale once again. Do your pre-shot routine and then execute. It's that simple.

---

During practice, most golfers will simply put a ball down and hit one after another. You never do that while you are playing an actual round of golf. When you are on the course, you go through a pre-shot routine and then hit the shot. When you are on the practice range, you need to go through the same pre-shot routine for every ball you hit. If you don't follow that same exact routine in practice, you won't have 'carry over learning.'

The more practice is made to mimic situations you face during an actual round, the more the transfer of learning takes place. So practice how you will physically hit your shots and practice how you will handle your adverse emotions as well. It will revolutionize the way you play the game – guaranteed.

## GREAT GOLF Tip

### Maximize Practice Productivity

Jackie Steinmann was the UCLA women's golf team coach for 22 seasons. Her teams won 5 Pac 10 and one national title. She was two time National College Coach of the Year. Here are her four best practice tips:

• *Practice in chunks.* Never work on one aspect of your game before moving on to the next. Master one step before you go to the next one. That is how people learn. Most people can't assimilate too much information at one time. It's a process of trial and error. View failure as an opportunity to do something differently.

You need to have a goal for each shot that you are practicing. Then you must put your full attention towards that goal.

• *Don't work past your attention span.* In other words, don't hit 50 or 100 balls in a row because there comes a point in which you are no longer paying attention to what you are trying to accomplish.

For golf practice, it is much better to spend 75% of your time on the short game because that is where the scoring is. 63% of your score is your short game. Why wouldn't you spend at least 63% of your time on the short game? Most people at the range, continually hit drivers. That's a huge mistake.

• *Practice successes.* You don't need to practice unsuccessful things. In putting, for example, you need to practice making putts, not missing putts. So when you are practicing putting if you miss putts from a certain distance then you need to get closer to the hole.

You build confidence this way. Golfers need to validate their own success. When you do something good in practice, you need to pat yourself on the back. It can be something as simple as smiling.

• *Validate good shots by anchoring.* Do some physical motion that gets you emotionally attached to that previous good shot. You will often see Tiger Woods shaking his fists after a good shot – which he is using as an anchor.

The goal is to build a library in your brain of good shots. Then, when you want to hit a shot that is similar to one that you have had success with in the past, you can recall that at any time.

"Traveling between tournaments I would mentally rehearse each hole of the upcoming course I would be playing - seeing in my mind exactly how I wanted to play each hole."

— Ben Hogan

"I never hit a shot, even in practice, without having a very sharp in-focus picture of it in my head first."

— Jack Nicklaus

## Chapter EIGHT

**VISUALIZING YOUR NEXT BEST ROUND TO MAKE IT A REALITY**

We began this book with a story about a prisoner of war who used mental imagery and visualization to improve his golf game. Now I want to teach you how to maximize the use of visualization to take your game to a higher level and lower your score.

Let me start with a story on the power of visualization (in a negative sense). In 1928, four young men were headed from New York to New Jersey on the subway to compete in a track meet between their college and one in New Jersey. They were the 400 Meter relay team. As they stood hanging onto the straps, one of the men suggested that each visualize his leg of the relay using his stop watch for timing purposes. Their goal would be to run each leg as close to ten seconds as possible. As they traveled, hanging onto the straps, they visualized each leg over and over, each runner performing to his peak. They reached the track and competed. They finished dead last. When they rested and began to discuss the race, they found that they were all so exhausted from having "run" their legs so many times between New York and New Jersey, they were too tired to run well in the actual competition!

Whether you call it imagery, visualization, or mental rehearsal, we are talking about using the mind to see yourself on the golf course - not just performing various shots but also going through what you experience during your next 18 holes.

Depending on your personality, level of patience and willingness to practice, you can use visualization techniques one of two ways.

1) Simple mental rehearsal involves seeing in your mind a few seconds before you attempt a shot exactly where you want to place the ball. More golfers are comfortable with this type of strategy.

2) To get the big benefit that our POW did, you will have to spend more time and effort coming up with a complete mental training plan that must be practiced at home.

Here are four critical pre-requisite components before you start your imagery training plan:

1) *Visualization should always be preceded by relaxation.* You have to be in a comfortable quite place before you begin.

2) *Selection of an event and skill to be imagined.* Visualization should be as realistic as possible. Incorporate the use of all senses and the course you will be playing and the actual shots you will attempt.

3) *The technique to be imagined should be brought into focus.* An internal perspective is necessary. (It's as if you are viewing your swing through your own eyes). In addition, any attempt to feel the movement is effective in enhancing the imagery exercise.

4) *Practice the skill in "real time," there is no need to speed up or slow the swing down.*

## Visualize Flawless Execution

When you visualize you should have a clear picture of your best swing being executed flawlessly. If you find watching your own swing being perfectly executed difficult, you can watch your favorite professional and mentally model your swing to fit the one closest to yours.

Performance improves because the mind cannot distinguish between an imagined or real experience. To your brain, a neural pattern is a neural pattern whether it is created by a physical act or a mental act. Your brain sends the message to the muscles and the muscles react.

For most players, a long visualization on the day of competition is not beneficial (except for a brief pre-shot and/or post shot editing – see Chapter 6). It may cause you to relax too much and not be keen enough for your peak performance. For most of us, visualizing works best during the days or weeks leading up to a specific competition.

It is most effective when used at least once a day at a time when you are relaxed and undisturbed for about 15 to 30 minutes. You may find that just before bed is a good time. On the other hand, it may be the worst time if visualizing excites and energizes you. Be willing to experiment for a short time to find the most effective time and situation each day to quiet yourself, relax and visualize.

Now let's take a look at some more specific details on getting an imagery training session going. First, write down your goals for the upcoming round (more next chapter on goal setting). Have your supporting affirmation statements firmly in mind. Now you are ready to begin creating the content for a specific visualization.

See in your mind's eye the whole process and routine of your golf event in competition in as much detail as possible. Visualize the competition area, the weather or the atmosphere, the temperature, the sounds, the smells... everything. Imagine yourself warming up, stretching, talking to friends, concentrating on your pre-game shots - everything you do when you are about to play a real round of golf. Feel yourself being totally relaxed, confident, and in complete control of your body and your mental state. If you notice that you are nervous, remember your affirmations - "I am strong and ready" and "I am relaxed and prepared" - and say them to yourself.

Imagine yourself beginning to compete, starting with any pre-game ritual. Notice everything you do, seeing it perfectly just the way you want it to be, just the way it should be done. If you make a mistake while visualizing your performance, go back, rewind, slow down the image in your mind, and do it over again, correctly, perfectly - exactly as you know it should be done.

Experience yourself achieving your goals with perfect control and tactical know how. Guide yourself through the whole event with perfection. See yourself being successful. Be aware of how it feels and what it looks and sounds like to succeed, to achieve your goal. Allow yourself to experience achievement and success completely and fully by seeing, hearing, and feeling it all.

See yourself blasting out of a bunker and holing the shot to save par. See yourself hitting the perfect approach shot and finish it off to make an 8 footer for birdie.

Think of simple key words or phrases you can recall while you compete. These could be words such as "strong," "relaxed," "confident," "smooth," "centered," and so on. If, while visualizing, you reach a point in your performance when you usually have trouble or self doubt, that is the time to use these key words or your affirmations. They will help you re-focus and concentrate on your goal and let go of the negative feelings and distractions into which you may slip.

**Using Mental Rehearsal to Control Anger**

Now let's look at how imagery training can work to help a common trait that many golfers struggle with on the course – losing our temper. You will even see professionals get so frustrated that will let out a string of expletives or chuck their clubs into the water after a poor shot.

Has losing your cool helped you play better? If so, you can skip this exercise and head to the next chapter. For the rest of us, here is an imagery routine that can help us better deal with anger during competition.

Think of the last time you were angry or really lost your temper on the course. Make a list of what typically makes you lose your cool or sets you off.

Acknowledge any feelings of anger you might have during a typical round - remembering the list of things that make you angry. See yourself in a situation where you would normally totally lose your temper.

Now, say your affirmations about your anger. For example:

- "I let go of my anger easily."

- "I am in control of myself on the course."

- "I am powerful and centered."

- "I easily let go of mistakes or missed shots."

- "I am mentally tough."

- "I am focused on the task at hand."

Begin to imagine yourself handling your anger in a calm, comfortable and powerful way. See, hear and feel yourself succeeding - handling your anger - feeling powerful and in control.

See and feel yourself strong and powerful by acknowledging your anger and letting go of it quickly. You will not let your anger ruin your next round. You are going on to succeed - knowing that you have what it takes to be successful and to overcome any obstacles, including any anger you might have. See yourself replacing feelings of anger on the course with feelings of competence and confidence.

This is something that won't happen overnight – especially if you struggle with your temper. But with practice and patience, you will learn to manage your anger.

---

# GREAT GOLF Tip 8

**7 Keys to Make Visualization Work for You**

In her book "*The Mental Athlete*', sport psychologist Dr. Kay Porter gives step by step instructions on writing a visualization plan.

Before you write an imagery training program for yourself to practice, ask the following questions: First, how does your competition begin? What happens when you are warming up on the range? The beginning part of your visualization should include focusing on your goal and the outcome you wish to achieve. It should include everything important up to the moment you begin to physically compete.

The middle part of the visualization should consist of the event itself: mentally practicing every shot you might have to hit: drives off the tee, fairway woods and irons, sand shots and putts. If you are very familiar with the course, you can see in your mind how you might play each potential shot – 1 through 18.

The final part encompasses all that happens after you have competed. This may include post round handshakes and greetings, rejoining your foursome in the clubhouse and finally leaving the course.

Here are 7 steps to write your own visualization:

1) Ask yourself, what do you see, hear, and feel when performing during a typical round of golf? Write it down in a journal style notebook.

2) Begin with arriving at the course, going through your normal pre-round preparatory routine.

3) Go into vivid detail about the event and your experience of it, including sounds, smells, colors, the weather, and the positive feelings about your body and mental state.

4) Imagine yourself being totally relaxed, confident, powerful, and in complete control of your mind and body. Include affirmations and key words that will help keep you under emotional control during your real performance.

5) Go through your whole round thinking of each significant shot you will face. Feel yourself swinging smoothly and executing each shot exactly the way you want it to turn out.

6) After you have finished a journal of a complete round, go back re-read and edit your visualization. Make the changes that will absolutely keep your mind where it needs to be from start to finish.

7) Consider dictating your completed visualization plan into a tape recorder and listen to it as you mentally rehearse your performance. Pick a quiet time and place where you won't be disturbed. First thing in the morning or before going to bed at night are usually good times. The ideal state to listen to the tape is relaxed but mentally aware.

*"The greatest danger for most of us is not that our aim is too high and that we miss it, but that we aim too low and we reach it."*
— *Michelangelo*

*"Obstacles are things a person sees when he or she takes their eyes off the goal."*
— *Anonymous*

# Chapter NINE

## ULTIMATE GOLF PSYCHOLOGY: 3 SURE FIRE METHODS TO LOWER YOUR SCORE

**Part 1—**
**Goal Setting Strategies to Improve Your Game Now and Forever**

It's a well-worn cliché that you have to set goals to be successful at any endeavor. Your golf game is no different. For goal setting to work most effectively, there are several areas you must examine about yourself and your approach to the game of golf.

There has been a tremendous amount of sport psychology research done on the subject of goal setting. For the first part of this chapter, I want to break down key findings for you to use to make you a better golfer—over the short and long run.

The first thing you need to examine is what type of goal setting personality style you have. There is one style that will work much better for you in the long run. Don't worry. If you have one of the two less effective personality styles, now is the time to change. The three main goal setting personality styles include:

- Performance oriented.

- Success oriented.

- Failure oriented.

Golfers of all skill levels who adopt Performance Oriented goals make learning, mastering specific tasks, and personal improvement their highest priority. Because Performance Oriented golfers adopt a problem solving approach to competition, they seldom perceive failure when unsuccessful. Instead, they develop new strategies or re-commit to old ones. They often demonstrate tremendous persistence in the face of adversity. Because they worry little about failure, they set difficult goals that require maximal effort and the development of problem solving strategies to reach their goals.

Success Oriented golfers place the highest priority on demonstrating competence by outperforming the competition. Basically, they want to make sure they beat the guys in their foursome or at least hit a few remarkable shots during the round. Because their goal orientation is so caught up in winning, they do not want to fail and usually set only moderately difficult goals and only exert a moderate degree of persistence in the face of failure.

Another example of the Success Oriented golfer is the person who can't wait to brag about the long drive they hit on 15 or how they holed it from the bunker at the 19$^{th}$ hole after the round. They lost, but they can still brag about those great shots to their buddies.

Unfortunately, less difficult goals will typically hold back Success Oriented golfers from getting as much from a goal setting program as their Performance Oriented counterparts.

Another downside of Success Oriented golfers is that their confidence level is likely to fluctuate greatly depending on competitive match-ups. For example, when facing tougher opponents they may start making excuses like, 'I didn't give it a full effort today. If I had, I would have won.'

Failure Oriented golfers place the highest priority on social comparisons and "how they are perceived to look on the course". They dislike goal setting because it requires confronting personal failure. When Failure Oriented competitors believe they can't be successful, motivation changes from striving to succeed to avoiding failure.

The first key to making goal setting work for you is simple. Change your goal setting style to Performance Oriented if Success Oriented or Failure Oriented is where you are now.

After the change, you are ready to move on to the second step to make goal setting have much more impact. Most golfers tend to place higher priority on product goals (e.g. winning a tournament or shooting a lower score for one single round of golf.) rather than process goals (e.g. hitting the ball in the fairway consistently at least 75 percent of the time or making greens in regulation a set percentage of holes).

Even though they receive less attention than more glamorous outcome oriented goals, *process-oriented performance goals* (particularly difficult short term performance goals, as well as practice, and conditioning goals) are generally more effective than are outcome objectives (e.g. winning this week's round).

Process-related goals are effective for three reasons: 1. They create a consistent focus on areas that need improvement in your game. 2. They develop more consistently optimal levels of challenge that enhance motivation (i.e. effort, intensity, and persistence). 3. They focus on more controllable aspects of performance, which allows you to take credit for your successes, which raises your self-confidence.

You should set both short and long range goals to provide direction. Short-term goals fuel motivation and self-confidence on a daily basis and focus behavioral choices you face every time you practice.

If you really want to improve your game, you need to focus on daily process oriented practice goals and their important role in skill development. It's not as exciting, but is more important to long-term performance enhancement than other things you will do in regards to goal setting.

The third step to make goal setting more effective is to get on a mission. As you think about your personal mission as a golfer, you should be able to answer three critical questions: 1) Why do you play? 2) What would you like people to say about the way you play the game? 3) What do you want to accomplish?

Answering why you play is critical because when you know why you play golf, it will help you battle through the hardships and frustrations that you will inevitably face. The more specific reasons you can come up with as to why you play the game, the easier it will be to motivate yourself to work on your game every day.

---

## 5 Questions to Make Goal Setting More Effective

Here are five great questions to help you motivate yourself using goal setting:

1) *What would you like to be able to do as a golfer that you can't do now?* Example: "Hit the ball 50 yards longer off the tee."

2) *How would your golfing performance improve when you achieve your goal?* Example: "I would have a much better chance at getting to more greens in regulation."

3) *What have you done to achieve it?* Example: "I have started a regular stretching exercise program and began twice weekly lessons with a local professional."

4) *What things may be holding you back from achieving your goal?* Example: "I don't follow through on what I'm being instructed by the professional and I quickly revert back to poor swing habits."

5) *What is your plan of action, or mission, for accomplishing your goal?* Example: "I will chart my practice sessions to see exactly what is happening each time I hit a practice shot."

"I will approach practice like I'm actually playing a round of golf by giving myself mental situations I will face." (see Chapter 7 for more details).

"I will write down my goals and post the results of my practice sessions to see how I am progressing on my effort to achieve them."

---

Here are two final keys to make your goal setting plan show incredible results:

1) **Set Short, Medium, and Long Range Goals**. Set daily, weekly, monthly, and year long goals.

"In today's practice session I will hit 6 drives in a row within ten yards of my average best landing in the fairway and make 6 putts in a row from eight feet."

"This week I will hit a total of 50 sand shots - with at least 40 of them landing on the green within 15 feet of the hole."

"This month I will practice my short game for at least 90 minutes out of every two hour practice session."

"By the end of the year I will lower my handicap five strokes." (Yes this is an outcome goal, but long-range goals need to be more outcome oriented and short-term goals more process oriented).

2) **Re-adjust Goals Upward.** Once you commit yourself to goal setting, watch out, you will amaze yourself with the results. Soon enough you will have to re-adjust your goals to reflect your new found improvements in your game.

*A word of caution.* Make sure you are very close to reaching your short and medium ranged goals before making them more difficult to obtain.

---

**Part 2—Slumpbusting**

Now I want to address the dark side of golf that no one likes to talk about. The dreaded performance slump. Sport psychologist Dr. Jim Taylor is a specialist in helping athletes in this area. Here is his list of 4 causes and 3 cures for slumps or sustained performance declines.

You fall into slumps for no apparent cause and come out of them for equally unclear reasons. There are two certain facts about slumps. 1. They are unavoidable. 2. Performance, in time, will return to normal levels.

Basically, there are four causes of slumps.

*Physical:* This is the most difficult cause to identify because there are so many problem areas. Fatigue due to overtraining, illness, injuries, vision or hearing loss, and nutritional deficiencies all can contribute.

*Technical:* A "technical" swing flaw is something many golfers obsess about. Technique includes the timing, movement, and execution of your golf swing. One slight change and your entire game can be negatively affected. Until the change is identified, the performance drop will persist.

*Equipment:* Technology will never replace good technique, but it can help when the equipment change fits you as a player. Golfers have a very fine balance between equipment, technique and physical process associated with timing and feel. Small changes in equipment can have a profound impact in your game – and many times it's not the outcome you desire.

*Psychological:* This includes performance-related problems and personal problems that occur away from the competitive area. Golfers misperceptions of their own performance level are a common problem leading to slumps.

One of the first things you should do when a slump hits is to take time off from the game. Stay away from the course and the practice environment for a week or two. Ease back into it after you feel better mentally.

There are 3 slumpbusting goal areas you must address to alleviate performance slumps:

1. **Return-to-form goal.** Determine the level of performance you wish to attain. If your game has really taken a downturn, set very small achievable goals to get your confidence back.

2. **Causal goal.** Identify the specific causes of the slump and make a list about what you plan to do about each cause.

3. **Practice training goals.** After you have taken some time away, detail a practice training plan you believe will resolve the slump. Consult with your professional or instructor to help work out the details.

## Part 3— The Psychology of Finishing Strong Every Time

How many times have you played a great round through 13, 14 or 15 holes only to fall apart at the end? If it's a hot day, physical fatigue plays a factor. But more often times than not, it is mental fatigue that gets the best of you.

Fear not because the rest of this chapter is written specifically for the golfer who can't "close the deal" and finish strong. Let's look at 8 different ways you can keep your wits about you and insure you don't steal defeat from the hands of victory:

1. *Change your mind set.* The greatest athletes of all time wanted to have the ball in their hands when the game was on the line. Michael Jordan always wanted the ball with two seconds left so he could take control and win the game for his team. Joe Montana thrived on the pressure of the impossible, e.g. directing the two minute drill the length of the field. The best athletes perform their best when their backs are up against the wall.

As a golfer, you can be Joe Montana or Michael Jordan – you can take control of a late round situation and finish strong. To do this, you must first develop an acceptance of how tough it will be and thrive on the challenge. Convince yourself that the late holes present an opportunity to show your stuff.

Go back to what we talked about in the very first chapter - "act as if". By pretending like you are one of the greatest players around who love pressure situations, it will soon happen for real.

2. *Make practices as pressure filled as possible.* This will have you better prepared to handle the tough situations that arise. For example, put the ball 7 feet from the hole and tell yourself that this putt will determine whether I beat my all time lowest score or not.

3. *Mentally rehearse strong closings.* On a daily basis, even if it's only for a few minutes, see yourself finishing your round exactly the way they would like it to turn out.

4. *Let go of your ego.* Never allow yourself to become overwhelmed by the negative influence of others. Tough it out. You may be playing with a group of sarcastic wise guys who will say things to throw your game off at the end. Forget about them and focus on your upcoming shot. Don't get into a verbal

war of words. Ultimately, let your performance on the course speak for itself.

5. *Keep your sense of humor.* Be willing to laugh at yourself. Life really is fun, and so is golf. Look for something to laugh about in anything negative that takes place.

6. *Decide in advance what you want.* Plan as much as possible. How do you want your round to finish? What do you need to do today and in the days ahead to move closer to your goals? What's the best way to respond to poor weather or rude playing partners? How will you react to poor shots as they occur? The more advance planning you do, the better.

7. *Use stress reducing exercises.* When you are feeling stressed toward the end of the round and tension is mounting, here are two quick exercises to reduce your stress. 1. *Shoulder shrug.* To relieve upper chest and shoulder tension, raise shoulders as high as you can, hold for a few seconds and drop them to a normal position. 2. *Rag doll.* For overall tension, stand with arms dangling loosely at sides and start to shake your hands, then your arms.

1992 Masters Champion Fred Couples is just one touring professional who makes great use of these same exercises. In fact, if you watch him long enough, you will catch him performing the shoulder shrug and rag doll to get his body in tune – both on the course and at the practice range.

8. *Practice breathing to be able to relax under pressure.* Lastly, whether you are nervous on the first tee or putting for a chance to be your club's champion, here is the best way to relax, breath deeply and keep your composure.

Gently take a breath through your nose, inhaling air deep into your lower lungs. Allow your belly to expand without effort as you gradually fill the upper sections of your lung cavity as well. Hold the breath for two to three seconds.

Next, slowly exhale through your nose... feel your belly contract as you do. Expel all of the air. Take a little longer to exhale that you did to inhale. Continue to breathe slowly.

With each breath, your belly should rise as you inhale and contract as you exhale. Do this for at least five to seven additional breaths. Feel yourself experience more and more relaxation with each breath.

---

## GREAT GOLF Tip

**15 Tour Secrets to Play Your Best Golf**

1. Play the round in your mind the night before which gives you an extra practice round. (See Chapter 8).

2. Make a list of things that you do especially well and say them out loud on the way to the golf course.

3. Get to the course one-hour ahead of tee time leaving enough time for personal things so that there is no rushing.

4. Leave all personal problems on the seat of the car. They will be there when you return.

5. Warm up the body and the mind on the practice area. Do not attempt to make mechanical swing changes. These can be worked on later.

6. Practice putting first, then hit balls on the range. Make your last practice shot a good one with the club you are going to hit on the first tee.

7. Commit to walking, talking and acting like a winner no matter what happens, right down to the body language. A good idea might be to think about your favorite golfer and act like he or she would act.

8. Make a good yardage book during the practice round keeping a record of clubs hit to the different targets.

9. Have a game plan and stick to it.

10. Commit to giving every shot 100%. Perform the best you can on each shot, one shot at a time.

11. Anchor the good shots. Pause 3 to 5 seconds after making a great shot and remember exactly how it felt. This will put the shot into your muscle memory. When a similar shot is coming up you can "pull it up" out of your memory before taking a swing.

12. Be positive about everything. Negativity will kill your game. Stay absolutely present oriented in your focus.

13. Be totally target oriented for the entire round.

14. Stick to your pre-shot routine on EVERY shot.

15. Play as if the match is being held at your favorite course with your favorite holes, favorite weather and favorite playing partners – no matter what the actual conditions are.

## The Ten Most Powerful Two Letter Words

*"If it is to be, it is up to me."*

## Chapter TEN

**DECISION OR ACTION: IN THE END, IT'S UP TO YOU**

Question: Will the techniques and the philosophies we've covered in this book work for you?

Answer: Absolutely!

But here's the important thing...

These strategies will only work if you work them.

Back in the late 1960's my friend Jeff was a high school runner and his hero was Jim Ryun. In 1965, Jim Ryun became the first high school student ever to run a mile under four minutes.

Jeff wrote Jim Ryun's coach and told him his dream of replicating Ryun's feat. A few weeks later the coach sent him Ryun's workout for the two months leading up to his historic run. Jeff was ecstatic – he had the secret right in his hands. He excitedly showed these workouts to everyone.

For the rest of the summer, Jeff read the workouts, analyzed the workouts and talked about the workouts. Jeff only made one mistake...

He didn't do the work-outs!

Here is a riddle that perfectly illustrates this very point:

Question: There are three frogs sitting on a log and one frog decided to jump off the log. How many frogs are left on the log?

Typical answer: Most people think the answer is "two." That's logical, but wrong.

Correct answer: There are three frogs sitting on a log. One frog decided to jump off the log. Just because the frog decided to jump off the log doesn't mean it did jump. There's a big difference between deciding to use the techniques we've been talking about and actually using them.

It will be of no use what so ever if you don't practice and work on changing your mind set on a regular basis.

---

Before you play your next round of golf, there are two more things I want you to do.

#1. Read the list of 36 power statements and inspirational quotes that closes this book the morning before you tee-off.

#2. Buy some red sticky dots from an office supply store. Place these dots where you'll see them before you play your next round. Put a dot on your golf bag or on your water bottle, etc. No one else will know about them.

These red dots will be your own personal peak performance reminders of what we've covered here. Every time you see these red dots, it will trigger your mind to remember how to think like a champion.

You know what Coke and Pepsi are, but why do Coke and Pepsi advertise every day on radio, television, in newspapers, magazines and on billboards? Because they know you need constant and continuous reminders to buy their product. If Coke and Pepsi know how powerful advertising is and spend so much money on it—maybe you should advertise for yourself.

These red dots will be your own personal advertisements to help you bring out the best that is in you!

## 36 POWER STATEMENTS TO LOWER YOUR SCORE TODAY

In closing, I've come up with 36 power statements to inspire a lower score at your next round of golf. Read this list before you leave for the golf course.

1. The best golfer doesn't win - the golfer that plays best does.

2. "You must love the greens you are playing on today." Gary Player

3. You can change your attitude quicker than you can change your swing or skill level.

4. There are no hopeless situations in golf.

5. "Golf is a game of recovery." Walter Hagen

6. Remember the 1980 U.S. Olympic hockey team.

7. "Where do you find motivation? You find it within yourself." Michael Jordan

8. H.O.P.E.= Hold On Possibilities Exist.

9. The greatest mistake a person can make is to be afraid of making one.

10. You can do your best even when you feel your worst.

11. If you're not nervous, you're not ready.

12. Just because you are worried doesn't mean you have to act worried.

13. Some of the greatest athletes of all time did their best when they were scared to death.

14. "The coward and the hero feel the same fear. They just react differently." Cus D'Amato

15. "The hero is no braver than the ordinary man. But he is braver for five minutes longer." Ralph Waldo Emerson

16. It's OK to be scared. Just don't be scared about being scared.

17. "Fear no opponent. Respect every opponent." Coach John Wooden

18. The only place "success" comes before "work" is in the dictionary.

19. "The greatest pleasure in life is doing what people say you cannot do." Walter Bagehot

20. You can choose to have the attitude, the intensity and put out the effort of a Michael Jordan or Tiger Woods.

21. When you loosen up physically, you lighten up mentally.

22. Once you release your mental emergency brake, you'll perform better than ever before.

23. "I have to win" and "I must win" create tension. "I want to win" creates energy.

24. There are no "must make" putts in golf.

25. Focus on execution, not outcome.

26. "Golf is a lot like a love affair. If you don't take it seriously, it's no fun. If you take it too seriously, it breaks your heart." Arnold Daley, Sports Writer

27. "Full effort is full victory." Gandhi

28. "Make the total effort even when the odds are against you." Arnold Palmer

29. "To give anything less than your best is to sacrifice the gift." Steve Prefontaine

30. Don't be careless – care less. Don't be careful – care less.

31. Be intense without being tense.

32. Get rid of the 14 killer words: "This is it," "It's now or never," "It's do or die," "There's no tomorrow."

33. Don't let up when ahead. Don't quit when behind.

34. "Winning isn't imperative, but finishing strong is." Coach Paul "Bear" Bryant

35. "Play like a champion today." Sign in the Notre Dame football locker room

36. "Its kind of fun to do the impossible." Walt Disney

# INDEX

Acting As If .................................................. 26, 31, 94
Adversity ............................................................. 31
Affirmation Statements ............................. 73, 81, 83
Ali, Muhammad ................................................... 23
Anchoring Shots ............................................ 77, 97
Anger .......................................................... 82, 83
Attention Span .................................................... 77
Attitude ................................... 13, 14, 19, 23, 27
Awareness .......................................................... 72

Ballesteros, Seve ................................................ 21
Beem, Rich .................................................. 27, 28
Brain Patterns .................................................... 81
Breathing .............................................. 62, 95, 96
British Open ....................................................... 16
Brooks, Herb ...................................................... 17

Caring (Too Much) ................................... 23, 45, 46
Choking ...................................................... 21, 43, 48
Cohen, Herb ....................................................... 46
Concentration ..................................... 48, 57, 60, 63
...Exercises for 63, 64
...Focus Point 60
...Power Words 64, 65
Confidence ......................................... 23, 71, 88, 89
...Acting Confident 24, 27
...And Composure 73
...And Practice 77
...Lack of 25
Control (Sense of) ......................................... 32, 58
Couples, Fred ..................................................... 95

Damon, Matt .................................................................... 25
Deniro, Robert ................................................................. 46
Distractions ............................................................... 32, 72

Emotional energy (managing) ............................................ 74
Execution ......................................................................... 41
...Flawless Execution 80

Fan movie ......................................................................... 46
Faxon, Brad ............................................................... 54, 55
Fear ..................................................................... 21, 27, 61
   With Irrational Attitude 42, 43
Finishing Strong ......................................................... 94, 95
Focus ......................................................... 45, 53, 58
...Outcome based 41
...Process based 42, 60
...Scoring 36, 37
...Winning 40, 43
Forgin's Creed ................................................................ 31

Goals and Goal Setting ............................................... 85-91
...Causal goals 93
...Process based 89
...Return to form goal 93
...Short and long range 89, 91
Goldberg, Dr. Alan ..................................................... 41, 48
Grand Slam ..................................................................... 30
Greatest Game Ever Played movie ................................ 18


Hagen, Walter ........................................................ 25, 105
Hogan, Ben ............................................................. 56, 78
Hope ........................................................................ 18, 27
Humor (Using to advantage) .......................... 28, 29, 95

Intensity (Levels of) ............................................ 51, 58, 73
Jones, Bobby .......................................... 18, 25, 52, 56, 57
Jordan, Michael .............................................................. 94

Journal .................................................................... 85

Key Words ..................................................... 59, 82
Killer Words .................................................... 47, 48
Kuehne, Hank ....................................................... 68

Lasorda, Tommy ................................................... 28
Legend of Bagger Vance movie ............................ 25
Lewis, Lennox ....................................................... 24
Loehr, Dr. James ................................................... 53
Lombardi, Vince .................................................... 42
Los Angeles Dodgers ........................................... 28
Love, Davis III ....................................................... 44

Masters ................................................................. 19
Mattea, Kathy ........................................................ 48
Mental Athlete book .............................................. 84
Mental Emergency Brake ................................. 33-41
Mental Rehearsal and Visualization ................. 79-85
Mental Toughness ........................................... 53, 54
Mickelson, Phil ...................................................... 42
Michelangelo ......................................................... 86
Mind set ........................................................... 27, 38
Miracle movie ........................................................ 16
Montana, Joe ........................................................ 94


Nerves (Nervousness) ............................... 25, 26, 28
Nicklaus, Jack ....................... 29, 32, 44, 65, 66, 78
New Mental Toughness Training book ................. 53
Norman, Greg ....................................................... 21

Palmer, Arnold ...................................................... 66
Paterno, Joe .......................................................... 68
Peale, Norman Vincent ......................................... 31
Performance Blocks ........................................ 43, 48
Pirozzolo, Dr. Fran ................................................ 67
Player, Gary ............................................. 30, 31, 105
Poor Shots (Recovering from) ......................... 43, 69

Porter, Dr. Kay .................................................................. 84
Practice ...................................................................... 67-77
...Performance Cylces 74,75
...Red, green, yellow analogy 70
Pressure .................................................................. 37, 94
Putting .................................................. 19, 26, 48, 54, 55, 61
...Must make putts 40
Power of Positive Thinking book .......................................... 31

Quimet, Francis ................................................................ 16

Rag Doll Exercise ............................................................. 95
Ravizza, Dr. Ken .......................................................... 68, 69
Relaxation .................................................................. 67, 80
Rickles, Don .................................................................. 28
Rose, Pete ..................................................................... 65
Routines .................................................................. 73, 97
  And rituals 57
Russell, Bill ..................................................................... 24
Ryun, Jim ....................................................................... 99

Self Talk (Self-inventory) ................................................ 70, 72
Shot (Shot-making) .................................................. 58, 59, 60
Shoulder Shrug Exercise ..................................................... 95
Simulation Training ............................................................ 62
Singh, V.J. ......................................................................19
Slumps (Slumpbusting) .......................................... 48, 92, 93
Sprague, Dr. Dennis ......................................................... 71
Sport Psychologist ......................................................... 38, 67
Sports Slumpbusting book .................................................. 48
Stargell, Willie ................................................................. 52
Steinmann, Jackie ............................................................ 76
Stroke of Genuis movie ..................................................... 52
Super Bowl .................................................................... 47

Taylor, Dr. Jim ................................................................ 92
Thought of the Day .......................................................... 69
Thought Stopping ............................................................. 49
Trevino, Lee ...............................................................29, 58
Trust ..............................................................................60

U.S. Olympic Hockey Team ................................................ 16, 17
U.S. Open ............................................................................ 31, 42, 68

Van de Velde, Jean ................................................................... 21
Vardon, Harry ........................................................................... 16
Vietnam War .............................................................................. 11

Watson, Tom .............................................................................. 62
Winning ........................................................................... 14, 15, 35
..."Must Win" situations ..................................................... 39, 45
Woods, Earl ............................................................................... 72
Woods, Tiger ............................................................ 20, 26, 27, 57, 72
Worry .................................................................... 21, 22, 27, 47

Zero Station .............................................................................. 69
Zimmer, Don ............................................................................. 50

*For additional copies of this book and other books by these authors check your local bookstore or favorite library.* For more information about the book and other golf tips or special discounts visit: *GoodtoGreatGolf.com* or
Call toll free, 1-877-GOLF-421.

For comments to the author, scheduling interviews or speaking engagements, contact through the *authors'* page at:
www.LegacyPublishingServices.com